Alain Reix

The Jules Verne *at the* Eiffel Tower

new recipes

Alain Reix

The Jules Verne *at the* Eiffel Tower

new recipes

Photographs by Edouard Sicot

HERSCHER

Préface by Paul Haeberlin
chef of « Auberge de l'Ill » at Illhausern, Alsace

Recipes by Alain Reix

Text by Néron Richer

Translated by Isabelle Deparis

In order to help you prepare the recipes presented by Alain Reix, we have classified them by difficulty, using the following code:

Level of difficulty

 *easy*

 *average*

 *difficult (or easy for accomplished cooks)*

The asterisk placed after certain words in the recipes refers to pages 146 to 152 where you will find either an explanation of a basic recipe or the definition of a culinary term (for example: chicken stock).*

Editor: *Brigitte Richon*
Graphics: **foli-o**

ISBN: 2-7335-0311-1

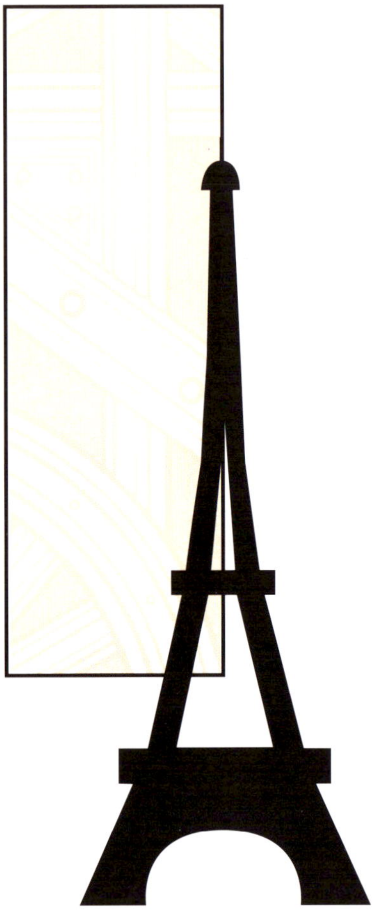

table of contents

My friend Alain Reix

Agadir, Bergerac, La Rochelle, Strasbourg, Paris, the Eiffel Tower… this has been the personal, professional and gastronomic journey undertaken by my friend, Alain Reix.

"You can't have real cookery without childhood memories ; not everything can be learned from textbooks and school. You often cook something because you want to recreate some moment from the past – a particular smell in the air or a flavour that your taste buds have never forgotten." Alain Reix uses all his memories in his cooking. From his birthplace of Agadir in Morocco come sardines, king prawns and honey-coated pigeons with warm spices and fresh mint. From the region of Périgord where his grandmother had a restaurant come the flavours of country cooking. His rural origins have also given him a taste for natural products of the earth and he willingly admits that he has a love of patés, sausages and meats prepared in the traditional way, not to mention the rich duck-liver paté which Périgord is famous for.

When he was sixteen, Alain already knew that he wanted to be a chef. He was very fortunate in being able to train under Jacques Le Divellac, a celebrated Breton chef who became Alain's spiritual father. During the eleven years that Alain spent in Jacques Le Divellec's kitchens, he learned not only all his master's secrets but also acquired the knowledge that would enable him to avoid the many pitfalls of his chosen profession.

It was in La Rochelle that Alain became skilled in the use of seafood and it was there too that he met Monique who was to become his wife, and the mother of their son, Julian.

In 1980, he made a move – to Alsace, where he decided to open his own restaurant, a modest establishment for no more than 25 diners. It was located in Schlitigheim, an industrial area just outside Strasbourg. This was where I met him for the first time and where he started to make a name for himself. He prepared dishes that he already knew and loved, not ones that came just from the region ; a bold move but one which paid off. He perfected his *terre-mer* style, which was to become his trademark : a harmonious combination of flavours from both sea and earth. He used spices from North Africa, truffles and terrines from Périgord and the savoury tastes of seafood, marrying them with sauerkraut, spätzels and freshwater fish. News of his skill spread from the local to the national press and it was not long before he obtained his first Michelin star.

In 1987, he felt he had to expand and he opened *La Table gourmande*, a few miles south of Strasbourg, with room for about 100 people. It was here that he found the need for different skills. A large restaurant with a staff of 20 needs to be managed by someone with great strength of character and excellent organisational abilities. The same high quality of cuisine must be maintained at all times and, although satisfied customers often return in the hope of renewing the gastronomic experience they had the time before, a successful restauranteur cannot rest on his laurels. He has to innovate and gradually persuade clients to try something new, and to help them discover new tastes. The reward is in their gratitude and, if you love to give people pleasure, that is the reward you seek.

Alain is just that sort of person – generous, outgoing and inventive but, above all he is a hard worker. He would spend hours in the kitchens of *La Table gourmande*, forever innovating and yet always basing his recipes on classic cooking methods, never going against the golden rule that had been handed down to him: respect the product you are working with.

His drive and hard work led him to accept a new challenge. In 1992, he was asked to come to Paris and take charge of the *Jules Verne* restaurant on the third floor of the Eiffel Tower. With his long experience behind him, he took on this new responsibility with enormous pleasure. Now, with a large staff at his command and 200 people to cater for at every meal, he undertakes this daunting task with calm and equanimity, never forgetting the culinary secrets learned so far away from his new home in the sky above Paris.

Paul Haeberlin

The Eiffel Tower : a gastronomic history

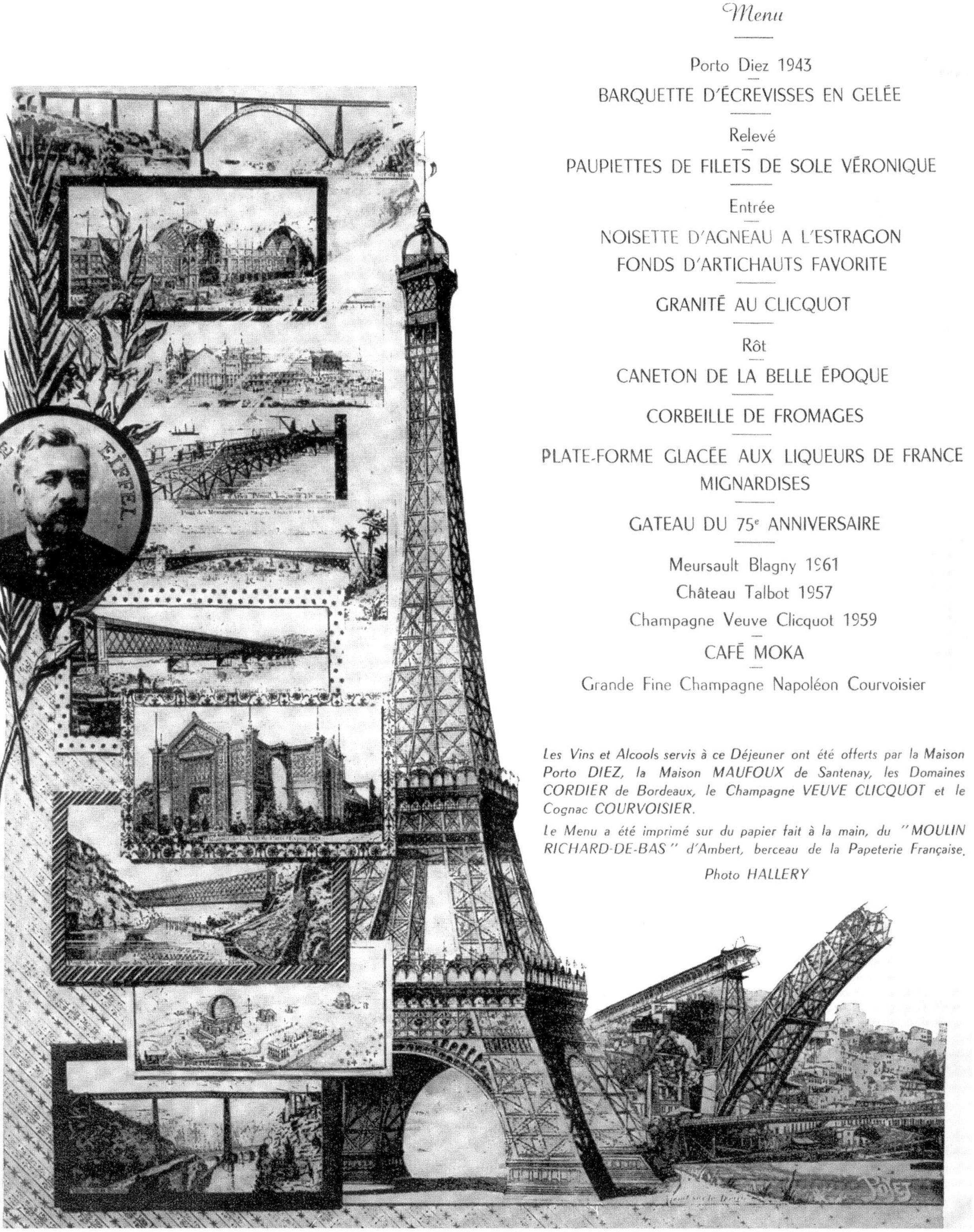

Menu

Porto Diez 1943

BARQUETTE D'ÉCREVISSES EN GELÉE

Relevé

PAUPIETTES DE FILETS DE SOLE VÉRONIQUE

Entrée

NOISETTE D'AGNEAU A L'ESTRAGON

FONDS D'ARTICHAUTS FAVORITE

GRANITÉ AU CLICQUOT

Rôt

CANETON DE LA BELLE ÉPOQUE

CORBEILLE DE FROMAGES

PLATE-FORME GLACÉE AUX LIQUEURS DE FRANCE

MIGNARDISES

GATEAU DU 75e ANNIVERSAIRE

Meursault Blagny 1961

Château Talbot 1957

Champagne Veuve Clicquot 1959

CAFÉ MOKA

Grande Fine Champagne Napoléon Courvoisier

Les Vins et Alcools servis à ce Déjeuner ont été offerts par la Maison Porto DIEZ, la Maison MAUFOUX de Santenay, les Domaines CORDIER de Bordeaux, le Champagne VEUVE CLICQUOT et le Cognac COURVOISIER.

Le Menu a été imprimé sur du papier fait à la main, du "MOULIN RICHARD-DE-BAS" d'Ambert, berceau de la Papeterie Française.

Photo HALLERY

Above: the Effeil Tower feast menu. Here, the meal offered the May 15, 1964.
Previous page: the *Russian restaurant,* built in 1889, on the first platform.

Gustave Eiffel was reputed to be a lover of fine food, and his gourmet's instincts were certainly with him when he designed and built the Tower that bears his name.

The building of the Tower

On 31st March, 1889, Eiffel gave a small party for his team of assistants and construction workers. He cared a great deal about the welfare of his employees and offered them a buffet with white wine under shimmering strands of lights. However, there was also a much more lavish party given for the French media. Eiffel knew the value of publicity and, before the inauguration of the Tower, he invited 150 influential members of the press to a magnificent luncheon on the first level, which was still under construction. The invitation specified that it was an informal affair, but judge for yourselves from the menu:

Truites à la gelée sauce verte

Tournedos à la Béarnaise

Homard à l'Américaine

Chaud-froid de poulardes

Ortolans sur canapés

Mousse de foie gras

Salade Vénitienne

Mazarines à la Montmorency

Gelée Victoria

All this was accompanied by various wines, champagnes, liqueurs and cigars. The huge success of the luncheon made Gustave Eiffel realise the appeal of sampling gastronomic delights high above Paris.

The 1889 World Fair

The inaugural dinner was held on May 15, 1889. No less than 19 dishes were served, from *Écrevisse Crème Saint-Germain* to *Glace Tour Eiffel*. There was wild boar Moscow-style, stuffed peacock, salmon, turbot, foie gras, feather-light pastries... From that moment on, dining out at the Eiffel Tower became the fashionable thing to do.

During the World Fair, some two million people visited the Tower. They came from near and far: not only from Paris and the French provinces but from all over the world, including royalty and other celebrities. And the climb up to the top left them all with an appetite.

Four 500-seater restaurants on the first level catered to the visitors' needs. There was an Alsace-Lorraine brasserie, a Russian restaurant, a British-American bar and, the best-known of the four, *Le Brébant*. This restaurant became the jewel in the crown of "Eiffelian gastronomy". Anyone who was anyone during *La Belle Époque* went there to dine and numerous anecdotes of the period are set in *Le Brébant*. It was there that a famous reconciliation took place: between Gustave Eiffel and Charles Gounod, who had been an unshakeable detractor of the Tower. Their meeting was witnessed by none other than Thomas Edison.

The biggest problem for the visitor to the World Fair was to find a place to eat. Everywhere was full to bursting and had lines of people waiting. Raoul Toché, in the *World Fair Magazine*, wrote: "You climb, you climb some more, and still more, but you don't feel exhausted because admiration strengthens the legs and the lungs. Then you arrive at last at the first platform, a Promised Land where the hand of God has been generous enough to set down some restaurants. Oh joy! A vacant table! Take it by storm! Waiter, please bring me a *beefsteak aux nuages* with *pommes à l'azur*".

In 1896, the Honourable Hung Tchang, an

Eastern plenipoteniary, who brought with him all the mystery of the Orient, had a very unusual meal there:

Croustades de Tche-Li

Filets de sole Tour Eiffel

Agneau au riz de Chine

Canetons de Rouen à la Tientsin

Cailles de Ho-Fei en chaud-froid

Écrevisses du Nigan-Hoei en buisson

Bombe Parisienne

Some sharp-tongued wag commented that the venerable mandarin hadn't touched any of the food because he suffered from vertigo.

From the 1900 World Fair to the Jules Verne

Some years passed, and the Eiffel Tower enjoyed continued success, as did its restaurants in the clouds. The World Fair in 1900 was the occasion for new gastronomic pleasures, and the installation of elevators also attracted diners who had previously been reluctant to make the climb. The elaborate banqueting tradition instituted by Gustave Eiffel was carried on by the many clubs and societies, both civil and military, who held their festivities there.

When the international exhibition of 1937 took place, the original restaurants looked a little dated and were replaced by two luxurious establishments decorated in pure 30s style. Then in 1949, a restaurant was opened on the second level – *En plein ciel* – which confirmed the Eiffel Tower's position as a place for good food and sophistication. It was there, on May 15th 1964, date of the 75th anniversary of the Eiffel Tower, that 75 Parisians of 75 years of age were invited to dine, among whom was the great Maurice Chevalier. On the menu was *Caneton Belle Époque*: a dish of duckling that was so delicious as to be unforgettable.

During the renovation of the Tower in 1980, two new establishments were built on the second level: a brasserie *La Belle France* and the *Altitude 95* restaurant. But the best was yet to come in 1983 when the *Jules Verne* was opened, with its own elevator. It is considered to be one of the finest tables in Paris, as you can judge from the following menu created for 14th July, 2000:

Terrine de foie gras de canard,
croustillant d'olives noires

Tartare de gros tourteaux,
gelée de concombre au caviar Sévruga

Tagine de homard aux oignons nouveaux et dattes

Selle d'agneau du Quercy, son jus monté aux
truffes d'été, pommes écrasées aux oignons grillés

Cabécou de Viellevie, salade aux amandes grillées

Baba au Rhum aux framboises

French gastronomy and the Eiffel Tower look forward to spending many more years in each other's company!

A section of the restaurant *Brébant*, built on the first floor, for the 1900 World Fair. The kitchens were suspended from the platform.

BREBAN
ECROT
CONSTRUCTEUR
PARIS

JULES
TOUR

The Jules Verne

One shall tread the air
As one treads the earth

At the entrance to the private elevator is the above quotation, taken from Jules Verne's *Robur The Conqueror*, welcoming visitors who come to lunch or dine.
It was at the beginning of the 1980s that the decision was taken to create a panoramic restaurant offering *haute cuisine* on the first level of the Eiffel Tower. The S.N.T.E (*Société nouvelle d'exploitation de la Tour Eiffel*) entrusted the architects and decorators Slavic and Loup with the task of creating a space where one can look out over the incomparable panorama of Paris and savor the very best in French cuisine. The *Jules Verne* was opened in 1983 and, in 1993, the Elior Group called on the services of Alain Reix, a chef then working in Alsace but whose origins were in the South of France.

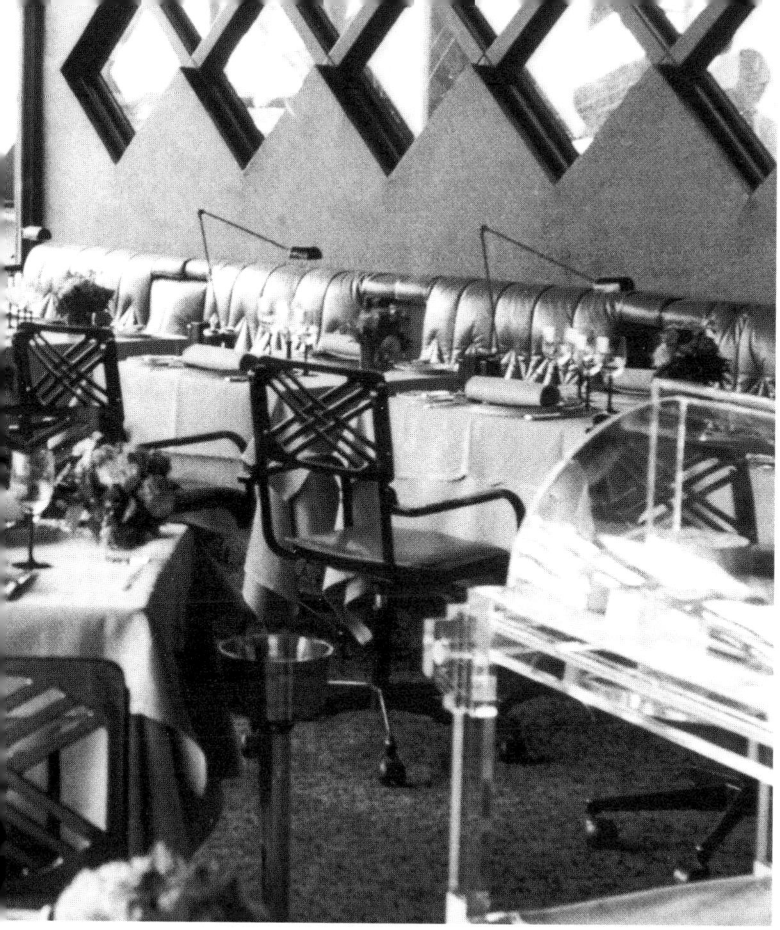

Every day, early in the morning, work begins in the Jules Verne as the dining-room staff, under the management of Arnaud Tachi, prepare for the two daily sittings. After checking that the tables are immaculately set and that the cutlery is glittering, they go through the menu with Alain Reix so as to be able to explain each dish to the guests. Everything is ready by a quarter past twelve when the first customers arrive. The barman pours the first glass of champagne and the gastronomic feast begins.

Recipes

1

starters

Caviar minestrone and tartare of cod

RECIPE PAGE 28

This dish is to be served cool, it blends Mediterranean tradition with the forceful taste of cod and the sharpness of caviar.

Caviar minestrone and tartare of cod

Difficulty: ♜♜

Preparation: 20 mn

Cooking time: 35 mn

Standing time: 30 mn

INGREDIENTS FOR FOUR PEOPLE

MINESTRONE
50 g carrots
50 g fennel
50 g celery
50 g celeriac
50 g turnips
50 g white of leeks
10 g chopped garlic
100 g crushed tomatoes*
20 g basil
2 dl olive oil
1 1/4 l chicken stock*

TARTARE OF COD
400 g cod fillet
1 minced shallot
1/2 bunch of chopped dill
4 tablespoons olive oil
100 g Seruga caviar

Salt
Freshly-ground pepper

Prepare the minestrone: wash the vegetables and cut a *brunoise* of carrot, fennel, celery, celeriac, turnip and white of leek. Prepare the crushed tomatoes*. In a skillet, brown the vegetables, tomatoes and garlic with the olive oil. Cover with the chicken stock*. Cook gently for 30 minutes. Set aside in the refrigerator.

Tartare of cod: finely dice the cod fillets. Peel and finely chop the shallot and chop the dill. Add to the cod with the olive oil and 60 g of caviar. Mix gently. Season. Set aside in the refrigerator.

When serving: place a *quenelle* of diced cod in the center of each soup plate. Pour in the cold minestrone and decorate with the remaining caviar and basil.

Wine advice: choose a white Hermitage, a particulary rich wine, because of the *roussane* and *marsane* grapes, which provide it with honeyed and candied flavors.

Lentil soup with scallops, calf's foot and fried bacon

Ingredients for four people

Difficulty:

Preparation: 20 mn

Standing time: 2 h 30

400 g lentils from Le Puy
1 l chicken stock*
2 carrots
2 leeks
1 head of garlic
2 onions
2 *bouquet garni**
200 g double cream
2 calf's feet
12 shelled scallops
50 g butter
12 slices of bacon

Salt
Freshly-ground pepper

Prepare lentils: peel 1 carrot, 1 leek, 1 onion and cut them into larges pieces. Put them in a saucepan with 1/2 head of garlic, 1 *bouquet garni**, lentils and the chicken stock*. Cook gently for about 1 hour. Blend and strain. Heat again and add the double cream. Cook for 2 minutes. Set aside.

Prepare calf's feet: meanwhile, put the calf's feet, the remaining onion, carrot, leek, bouquet garni and garlic in a large saucepan. Pour in 2 l of water. Cook for 2 hours and a half. Remove the calf's feet and bone them. Dice into small cubes. Set aside.

Before serving: heat the butter and sauté the scallops for 2 minutes on both sides. Drain and set aside. Brown the bacon slices in a frypan and set aside.

When serving: place a spoonful of diced calf's foot on each plate. Add 3 scallops, some lentil soup and top with bacon. Serve at once.

Wine advice: choose a spicy and sunny wine, such as a red Bandol.

Baskets of steamed oysters with fennel and lemons

RECIPE PAGE 32

When you lift up the lid, you are greeted by a smell of the sea. These slightly warm Marennes oysters go perfectly with fennel and lemon.

Baskets of steamed oysters with fennel and lemons

Difficulty: A

Preparation: 20 mn

Cooking time: 10 mn

INGREDIENTS FOR FOUR PEOPLE

24 oysters (N° 2 special)
1 handful of seaweed
15 cl olive oil
1 bunch of basil

STEWED FENNEL WITH LEMON
1 large fennel
100 g butter
200 g crushed tomatoes*
1 preserved lemon

Salt
Freshly-ground pepper

4 steaming baskets (25 cm in diameter) with lids

Prepare stewed fennel with lemon: dice the fennel. Heat the butter in a skillet and add the fennel. Braise gently. 5 minutes before the end of cooking, add the crushed tomatoes*. Blend the preserved lemon and mix in the vegetables. Season. Set aside.

Before serving: remove the oysters from their shells. Set aside and keep the shells. Drain. Place some seaweed and the shells in each steaming basket. Fill them with the stewed fennel and one oyster. Stack the four baskets and boiling water in a large skillet. Cover the baskets with lids. Cook for 2 minutes. Mix olive oil with the chopped basil. Set aside.

When serving: remove the lid and pour a teaspoon of olive oil mixture on each basket. Cover and place on 4 plates. Serve at once.

Wine advice: this bold match of oysters, fennel and lemon requires the tangy grapefruit notes of Jurançon wine.

Spinach salad with salmon and salmon butter

Ingredients for four people

Difficulty: (2 out of 3)

Preparation: 20 mn

Cooking time: 12 mn

600 g salmon fillet
3 kg young spinach leaves
250 g butter
160 g salmon roe
1 bunch of chives
Juice of 1 lemon
Salt
Freshly-ground pepper
Cayenne pepper

Tinfoil
Clingfilm

Prepare the salmon: remove skin and bones. Split each fillet and open it up to from a square shape. Roll tightly and wrap in clingfilm to hold the cylinder shape. Set aside in the refrigerator for 30 minutes. Cut the salmon roll into 4 pieces and remove the clingfilm. Heat 50 g butter in a skillet and cook for 2 minutes. Preheat the oven to 460 °F (240 °C, gas mark 8) and bake for 8 minutes. Keep warm.

Prepare spinach salad: wash baby spinach leaves and drain them. Set aside 1 kg. Heat 60 g butter in a skillet and cook the remaining spinach for 30 seconds. Drain.

Prepare the salmon butter: place the softened butter, salmon roe, chopped chives, the lemon juice, freshly-ground pepper and Cayenne pepper in a salad bowl. Mix well. Roll the mixture in tinfoil and set aside in the refrigerator.

When serving: mix the raw and cooked spinach together. Place it on 4 hot plates, add the salmon. Remove the tinfoil from the salmon butter and slice it. Place slices of butter around spinach. Bake for 1 minute, in a hot oven. Serve at once.

Wine advice: a Mercurey 1er Cru, if possible vintage 1995. Its light herb-scented flavour emphasizes the blend of flavors in the recipe.

Lobster salad with baby vegetable ratatouille

RECIPE PAGE 36

Baby vegetables are the perfect accompaniment to the « Prince of Seas ».

Lobster salad with baby vegetable ratatouille

Difficulty: ♜♜

Preparation: 25 mn

Cooking time: 55 mn

INGREDIENTS FOR FOUR PEOPLE

4 lobsters (about 400 g each)
100 g butter
3 tablespoons olive oil
16 slices of zucchini
16 slices of egg-plant
8 dried tomatoes*

BABY VEGETABLE *RATATOUILLE*
1 zucchini
1 egg-plant
1 onion
1 clove of garlic
3 tablespoons olive oil
50 g butter

OLIVE OIL WITH DILL
1/2 bunch of dill
6 tablespoons olive oil

Salt
Freshly-ground pepper

Cut the lobsters in half: sauté them with the heated butter, in a skillet. Preheat the oven to 460 °F (240 °C, gas mark 8) and bake for 4 minutes. Shell lobsters, claws and tails. Set the carcass aside.

Prepare sliced vegetables: heat 3 tablespoons olive oil in a skillet. Sauté the sliced zucchinis. Drain and set aside. Do the same for the sliced egg-plants.

Prepare the baby vegetable *ratatouille*: peel and dice the vegetables. Heat the olive oil and butter in a skillet and sauté the vegetables. Turn down the heat and let simmer for 45 minutes. Season and set aside.

Prepare the olive oil with dill: finely chop the dill. Mix it with the olive oil in a bowl. Season.

When serving: make alternate circles of dried tomatoes*, slices of zucchini and egg-plant. Place a spoonful of *ratatouille* in the center, top with shelled lobsters. Decorate with the red lobster's carcass. Spinkle with the olive oil with dill and serve warm.

Wine advice: choose a noble wine: a Puligny-Montrachet. Such a rich, full-bodied, ample and expressive wine is a fitting complement to this recipe.

Tartare of langoustine and cucumber with fresh cream cheese

Ingredients for four people

Difficulty:

Preparation: 15 mn

Standing time: 1h30

24 large *langoustines*
4 shallots
1/2 bunch chives
4 tablespoons olive oil
Juice of 2 lemons
4 tomatoes

Fresh cream cheese with cucumber

2 cucumbers
1 bunch of dill
4 mint leaves
5 tablespoons of fresh cream cheese (40 % full fat)

Salt
Freshly-ground pepper
Coarse salt

Prepare the *langoustines*: peel and finely chop the shallots and chives. Shell the *langoustines* and dice them. Mix the diced *langoustines* with shallots, chives, olive oil and lemons juices. Set aside in the refrigerator, for 1 hour at least.

Prepare the cucumber with fresh cream cheese: peel the cucumbers and remove the seeds. Grate them and sprinkle with the coarse salt. Set aside for 1 hour. Drain. Rinse and strain through muslin until well drained. Chop the dill and mint. Mix the cucumbers with the dill, mint and the fresh cream cheese. Season. Set aside in the refrigerator.

Prepare tomatoes: peel the fruit, remove the seeds and dice. Season. Set aside.

When serving: place a large spoonful of cucumber in the center of each plate. Add a spoonful of diced tomatoes. Arrange three *quenelles* of tartare of *langoustines* around it. Serve cool.

Wine advice: accompany this starter by a rare and interesting candied-fruit scented wine: a white Châteauneuf-du-Pape.

Marinaded sardines and fried foie gras

RECIPE PAGE 40

The extremes of taste, the tang of sardines, and the smoothness of *foie gras*. Serve it with curly endive, olive oil, chives and chervil.

Marinaded sardines and fried foie gras

Difficulty : A A

Preparation : 20 mn

Standing time : 30 mn

Cooking time : 2 mn

INGREDIENTS FOR FOUR PEOPLE

12 sardines
4 tablespoons olive oil
Juice of 2 lemons
4 escalopes of duck *foie gras* (about 60 g each)
1/2 bunch of chives
1 teaspoon of *appétits**

Salt
Freshly-ground pepper

Paper towel

Prepare the sardines : cut the tails, gut and wash the fish. Remove the fillets with great care. Place the fillets on a dish and mix the olive oil and lemon juice. Brush the fish and let them marinate for 30 minutes. Drain but keep the marinade.

Before serving : chop up the chives. Heat the skillet and fry the escalopes of *foie gras* for 2 minutes on both sides, on high heat. Season and set aside on the paper towel.

When serving : arrange the sardines like spokes of a wheel. In the center of each plate place a slice of *foie gras*. Add a dash of marinade and some chives on the sardines. Sprinkle *appétits** on the *foie gras*.

Wine advice : this starter goes well with a Pouilly-Fuissé and its tangy taste.

Pressed herrings with gherkins and potatoes with truffles

RECIPE PAGE 44

Sea and land rub shoulders in this unusual combination of flavors and textures.

Pressed herrings with gherkins and potatoes with truffles

Difficulty: ♜♜♜

Preparation: 30 mn

Cooking time: 15 mn

Standing time: 12 h

Ingredients for twelve people

24 rollmops
1 kg potatoes (Rattes du Touquet)
2 large apples
10 Russian-style gherkins
8 sheets of gelatine
600 g double cream

Salt
Freshly-ground pepper

A rectangular cake tin (25 cm in kength)
Clingfilm

For a decorative-looking terrine
500 g potatoes
2 truffles

Olive oil with dill
4 tablespoons olive oil
1/2 bunch of dill

Prepare the terrine: cook the potatoes in boiling salted water. Peel the apples and slice thinly. Cut the gherkins lengthwise. Set aside. When the potatoes are cooked, set aside 500 g of them and slice the remaining ones lengthwise. Soak the sheets of gelatine in the cream and heat on a medium heat for a few minutes. Leave to cool down while you prepare the terrine.

Prepare the terrine: line the mould with clingfilm. First place a layer of rollmops then, in turn, a layer of gherkins, apples, potatoes and a large tablespoon of gelatine and cream mixture. Repeat three times, ending with rollmops and then pour over the gelatine mixture. Wrap clingfilm over the terrine. Leave in the refrigerator for 12 hours.

Prepare the olive oil with dill: in a bowl, mix the oil with the chopped dill.

When serving: slice the remaining potatoes and the truffles. Arrange into a ring on each plate. In the center, place a slice of terrine. Pour some olive oil with dill over the potatoes.

Wine advice: to match the strong rollmops taste, choose a great wine from Côte de Beaune: a Meursault.

Rosette of langoustines, olive and tomato tart

RECIPE PAGE 48

The subtle taste of *langoustines* blended with tomatoes, Italian style.

Rosette of langoustines, olive and tomato tart

Difficulty: 🗼🗼

Preparation: 15 mn

Cooking time: 6 mn

Standing time: 3 h

Ingredients for four people

16 large *langoustines*
8 teaspoons of pesto (basil sauce)
8 teaspoons olive oil
Basil leaves

Olive and tomato tart
15 cl water
15 g caster sugar
10 g salt
30 g baker's yeast
50 black olives
500 g flour
100 g olive oil
600 g crushed tomatoes*
6 candied tomatoes*

Salt
Freshly-ground pepper

Prepare the tart: mix the water, sugar, salt, baker's yeast and chopped black olives. Add the flour and the olive oil. Knead well. Place in the refrigerator for 3 hours. Roll out the dough and cut 4 round disks (8 cm in diameter). Put them on a oiled baking tray, place in an oven preheated to 350 °F (180 °C, gas mark 5) and bake for 4 minutes. When serving, cover with crushed tomatoes* and top with slivers of candied tomatoes*.

Prepare the *langoustines*: shell the *langoustines* and keep only the tails. Pour 2 tablespoons of water into a soup plate. Put in the *langoustines*, season and cover with clingfilm. Bake in the microwave for 2 minutes. Drain and set aside.

Prepare the pesto flavoured olive oil: mix the pesto with the olive oil in a bowl. Season and set aside.

When serving: place a tart on each plate with 4 *langoustines*. Sprinkle on the flavoured oil. Decorate with a few basil leaves. Serve warm.

Wine advice: choose a white Savigny, a rare and elegant wine from Côte de Beaune, with citrus fruit notes.

Free-range pigeons and marinaded tuna, sauerkraut salad

Difficulty: ▲▲▲

Preparation: 30 mn

Cooking time: 2 h

Standing time: 10 mn

Ingredients for four people

4 good-sized pigeons
6 tablespoons goose fat
600 g fillet of tuna

Sauerkraut salad
8 tablespoons beer
1 egg yolk
8 tablespoons walnut oil
350 g raw shredded cabbage
1 teaspoon of cumin

Lemon vinaigrette
6 tablespoons olive oil
Juice of 2 lemons

Salt
Freshly-ground pepper

Prepare the pigeons: bone them and set aside the whole fillets. Cook the legs in the goose fat for 2 hours. Remove the skin from the fillets and finely mince them. Set aside.

Prepare the sauerkraut salad: blend the egg yolk and the beer for 30 seconds. Add the walnut oil. Season. Place the shredded cabbage in a salad bowl. Mix with half of the beer vinaigrette and sprinkle on the cumin. Set aside.

Prepare the lemon vinaigrette: mix the olive oil with the lemon juice. Season. Set aside.

When serving: thinly slice the tuna and line 4 plates. Place some minced fillets and two pigeon legs in the middle. Brush the tuna and the pigeons with the lemon vinaigrette. Leave for 10 minutes. Add the seasoned cabbage and sprinkle with the remaining beer vinaigrette. Serve cold.

Wine advice: choose a Pommard, a rustic, full-bodied wine. Try an old vintage; you will enjoy its subtle aromas.

Snail pastillas and oyster sauce

RECIPE PAGE 54

Moroccan scents, snails from the Charentes region and Marennes oysters : a mix of cultures.

Snail pastillas and oyster sauce

Difficulty : ♜♜♜

Preparation : 30 mn

Cooking time : 10 mn

Ingredients for four people

400 g small shelled snails
6 eggs
1 teaspoon of five spices
40 g raisins
40 g pistachio nuts
40 g crushed almonds
200 g fresh mint
100 g dried apricots
250 g butter
12 sheets of phyllo pastry
150 g clarified butter
1 tablespoon icing sugar
200 g rocket salad

Oysters vinaigrette
6 oysters
12 tablespoons olive oil
4 teaspoons of wine vinegar

Salt
Freshly-ground pepper

4 individual cake tins of 10 cm

Prepare the snail stuffing: beat the eggs in a bowl until you obtain a smooth mixture. Add the spices, raisins, pistachio nuts, crushed almonds, chopped mint, apricots and softened butter. Mix gently. Rinse and drain the snails. Add them to the egg mixture. Set aside.

Prepare the pastillas: brush 3 sheets of phyllo with the clarified butter. Put them on top of each other and cut a first circle 15 cm in diameter and a second 10 cm in diameter. Place the larger one in a cake tin and fill with snail stuffing. Fold the phyllo over the snail stuffing and top with the smaller circle of phyllo. Brush with clarified butter. Do the same for the other pastillas. Preheat the oven to 400 °F (200 °C, gas mark 6). Bake for 10 minutes. Unmold and sprinkle with icing sugar. Place under the grill for few seconds until the pastillas are browned.

Before serving: wash the rocket salad. Set aside. Prepare the oyster vinaigrette : shell the oysters. Blend them with the oil, vinegar, salt and pepper. Mix the salad and oyster sauce in a salad bowl.

When serving: place a handful of seasoned rocket salad and one pastilla on each plate. Serve hot.

Wine advice : choose a Bordeaux wine, rich and forceful, such as a Saint-Estèphe.

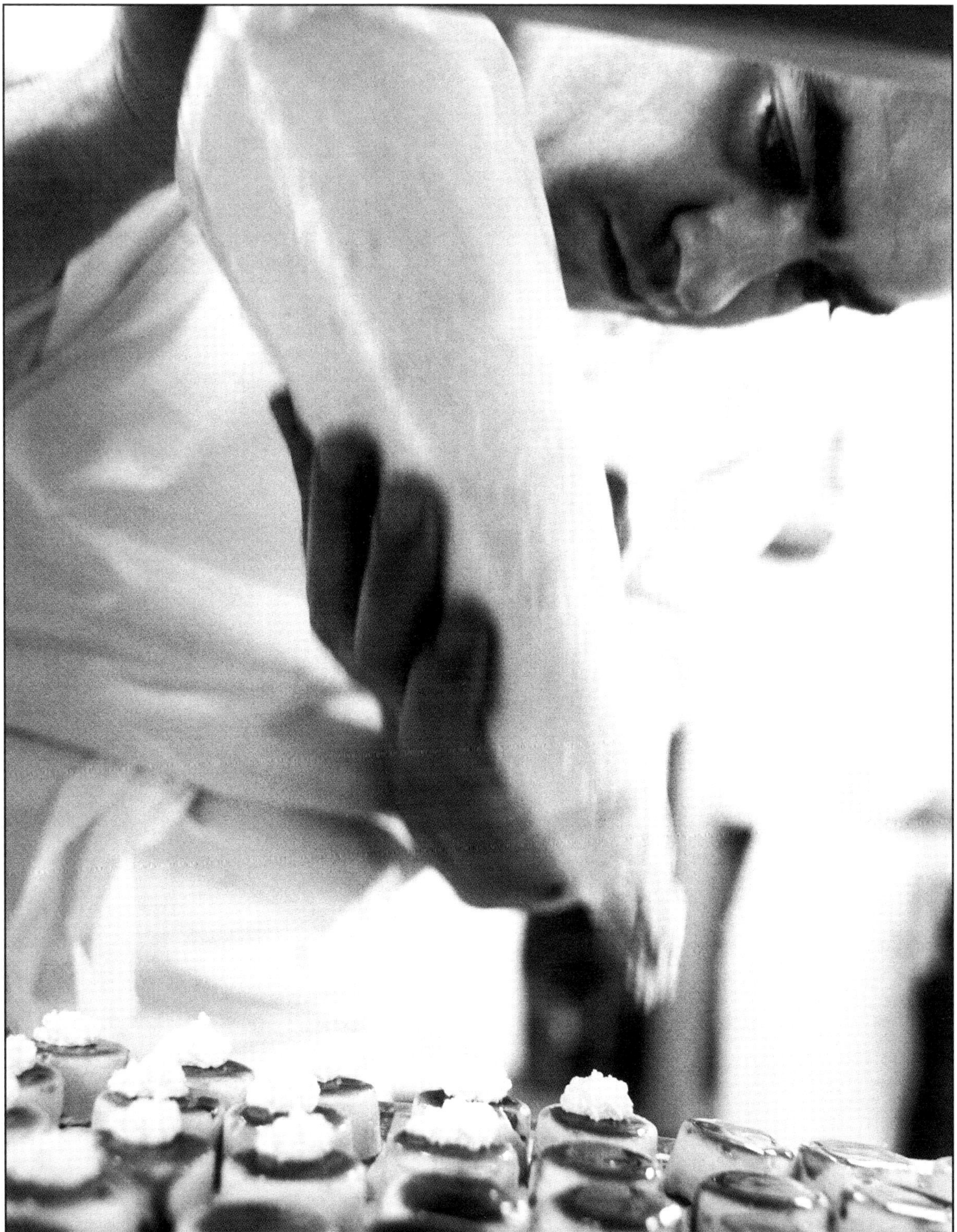

2

fish

Langoustines with salsify and grapes

RECIPE PAGE 60

This much-neglected vegetable is used here to match the subtle taste of *langoustines*.

Langoustines with salsify and grapes

Difficulty:

Preparation: 30 mn

Cooking time: 30 mn

Ingredients for four people

16 *langoustines*
1 kg salsify
3/4 l chicken stock*
90 g butter
1 kg white grapes
4 eggs

Salt
Fresly-ground pepper

Paper towel

Crisp potatoes
5 potatoes
2 tablespoons oil

Prepare crisp potatoes: peel and finely slice the potatoes. Lay them on a paper towel. Cook in the microwave for 3 minutes. Just before serving, fry them very quickly on both sides in a skillet, in oil.

Prepare salsify: peel and cut the salsify into 7 cm sticks, which you will cut lengthwise into 4 pieces. Boil the chicken stock* and cook the salsify for 10 minutes. Drain and keep the stock. Fold in 30 g butter. Reduce by 3/4. Season. Set aside.

Prepare grapes: peel grapes and remove the seeds. Heat 30 g butter in a skillet. Brown grapes for 2 minutes. Set aside.

Prepare *langoustines*: shell the *langoustines* and keep only the tails. Heat 30 g butter in a skillet. Sauté *langoustines* for 2 minutes on both sides.

When serving: place the salsify and grapes on each plate like a fan. Add *langoustines* and crisp potatoes. Pour over some sauce.

Wine advice: a Chablis *1er Cru*, if possible the excellent 1989 vintage, with its subtle flavours.

Omelette with shellfish and tiny crab sauce

Difficulty: A A

Preparation: 30 mn

Cooking time: 35 mn

Ingredients for four people

1 kg periwinkles
1 kg whelks
1 kg cockles
1 kg clams
16 eggs
1 tablespoon butter

Salt
Freshly-ground pepper

Skillet (12 cm in diameter)

Tiny crab sauce
3 kg small crabs
2 carrots
1 onion
1 leek
4 tablepoons olive oil
1 head of garlic
3 tablespoons tomato concentrate
1 l dry white wine
150 g butter

Prepare shellfish: boil 2 l of salted water. Plunge the periwinkles in boiling water and drain. Plunge the whelks in and drain. Shell and set aside. Put the cockles and clams on the baking tray and bake few minutes, until they open. Shell and keep warm.

Prepare tiny crab sauce: set aside 4 tiny crabs and crush the others. Peel and slice the carrot, onion and leek. Brown the vegetables, crushed garlic and small crabs in olive oil in a large pan. Add the tomato concentrate, the dry white wine and 1/2 l of water. Reduce by three-quarters. Strain. Add the butter and whisk. Set aside.

Prepare the omelettes: beat the eggs in a large bowl. Heat the butter and prepare 8 thin omelettes, just cooked. Keep warm.

When serving: place an omelette on each plate. Add a large spoon of shellfish and top with another omelette. Decorate with remaining tiny crabs. Serve hot.

Wine advice: a subtle and famous wine, a white Sancerre, will be a good match for this seafood dish.

Lettuce stuffed with crab

RECIPE PAGE 66

The lettuce is the queen of salads: the only one you can savour poached as well as braised. It deserves the marvellous meat of the *tourteau*, the king of crabs.

Lettuce stuffed with crab

Difficulty : ♦♦

Preparation : 20 mn

Cooking time : 50 mn

Ingredients for four people

4 lettuces
1 leek
1 carrot
2 cloves of garlic
100 g butter
50 cl meat glaze*
50 cl veal stock*
8 spinach leaves
8 tablespoons of olive oil
4 parmesan crisps*

Salt
Freshly-ground pepper

CRAB STUFFING
1 bunch of chives
4 leaves of mint
1 leek
1 stick of celery
50 g butter
500 g shelled crab

MINI- RATATOUILLE
1 red pepper
1 green pepper
1 yellow pepper
1 zucchini
1 egg-plant
1 onion
2 tablespoons olive oil

Prepare the mini-ratatouille : peel the vegetables and cut them into a *brunoise*. Heat the olive oil in a skillet and brown each vegetable separatately. Drain and mix. Set aside.

Prepare the crab stuffing : finely chop the chive and mint. Peel and thinly slice the leek and celery. Heat the butter in a skillet. Sauté the vegetables for 2 minutes. Remove from the heat before adding the shelled crab. Set aside.

Prepare lettuce : wash the lettuces whole. Blanch them for 1 minute. Drain well. Peel and thinly slice the leek, carrot and garlic. Put the butter and vegetables on the oven pan and brown them quickly on high heat. Preheat the oven to 420 °F (210 °C, gas mark 7). Remove from the heat, add the lettuces, meat glaze* and veal stock*. Bake for 45 minutes. Baste evenly from time to time. In the meantime, blanch the spinach leaves. Spread them out on a paper towel. Remove the pan from the oven. Keeping the juice, drain the lettuces. Open them with care, fill with the crab stuffing and fold. Wrap up each lettuce in two spinach leaves. Keep warm. Strain the cooking juice and reduce by three quarters. Season.

When serving : place 2 tablespoons of mini-ratatouille and a stuffed lettuce on each plate. Surround with sauce, add a dash of olive oil and a parmesan crisp*. Serve hot.

Wine advice : choose a dry Quincy, from the left bank of river Cher.

Fried shellfish and truffle-flavoured sausage

RECIPE PAGE 70

The best way to cook this is in a cast-iron skillet, like my grandmother used.

Fried shellfish and truffle-flavoured sausage

Difficulty: ♜♜♜

Preparation: 20 mn

Cooking time: 10 mn

Ingredients for four people

8 king prawns
4 tablespoons olive oil
300 g cleaned cuttlefish
4 scallop centres
8 clams
8 round clams
16 cockles
1/2 l mussel gravy*
2 tablespoons truffle juice

4 Individual cast-iron skillets

Truffle-flavoured sausage
1 small truffle
400 g sausage meat
200 g caul casing
30 g butter
3 tablespoons hazelnut oil

Salt
Freshly-ground pepper

Prepare the truffle-flavoured sausage: chop the truffle and fold sausage meat. Cut the caul casing into 4 small 8 centimeter squares. On each square, place a quarter of the mixture. Fold the sausage into a small thick pancake shape. Heat the butter and oil on medium heat. Cook for 3 minutes on both sides. Set aside.

Prepare the prawns: pan-fry the king prawns for 3 minutes on both sides in olive oil. Drain and set aside. Pan-fry the cuttlefish for 2 mn, drain and set aside.

Prepare the shellfish: pan-fry the scallops for 2 minutes on high heat, in the olive oil. Drain. Preheat the oven to 460 °F (240 °C, gas mark 8). Place the shellfisch on an oven tray and heat in the oven until they open.

When serving: place a sausage package in each skillet and put the shellfish, king prawns, scallops and shelled mussels around it. Add the mussel gravy* and truffle juice. Cover. Bake for a few minutes in the oven. Serve hot, in the skillets.

Wine advice: to let out the flavors of the prawns and shellfish, choose a generous wine: a white Graves.

Sesame king prawns, spinach purée and Béarnaise

RECIPE PAGE 74

Béarnaise prepared with Italian olive oil to accompany king prawns with the Mediterranean taste of sesame.

Sesame king prawns, spinach purée and Béarnaise

Difficulty :

Preparation : 10 mn

Cooking time : 10 mn

Ingredients for four people

12 large king prawns
3 kg fresh spinach
200 g butter
1 tablespoon double cream
200 g sesame seeds
200 g olive oil *Béarnaise**

Salt
Freshly-ground pepper

4 skewers

Prepare spinach : wash and blanch for 5 minutes. Drain well. Blend and strain. When serving, heat with 100 g butter and the double cream.

Prepare king prawns : shell the prawns and keep the tails. Put 3 prawns on each skewer and roll them in the sesame seeds. Heat 100 g butter on a high heat. Cook the prawns for 2 minutes on both sides.

When serving : place some spinach purée on each plate. Top with a skewered prawn. Serve at once, with olive oil *Béarnaise**.

Wine advice : choose a rare wine from Côte de Nuits : a white Morey-Saint-Denis.

Bream with mini-leeks and thyme

Ingredients for four people

Difficulty: ♜♜

Preparation: 10 mn

Cooking time: 25 mn

Standing time: 2 h

4 bream fillets (about 180 g each)
1/2 raw beetroot
32 mini-leeks
1/2 bunch chives

Shrimp sauce
3/4 chicken stock*
300 g shrimps
4 teaspoons thyme flowers
100 g butter

Salt
Freshly-ground pepper

Prepare vegetables: cut the beetroot into julienne pieces. Soak for 2 hours in the refrigerator. Boil 2 l salted water and cook mini-leeks for 10 minutes. Drain and cool under cold running water. Set aside.

Prepare shrimp sauce: pour the chicken stock* into a large saucepan. Add the shrimps, thyme and butter. Reduce by three quarters. Strain and season. Keep warm.

When serving: thinly slice the bream fillets. Put on four plates. Lay on the mini-leeks in criss-cross layers. Preheat the oven to 480 °F (250 °C, gas mark 8). Cook for one minute. Pour on the boiling shrimp sauce. Sprinkle the choped chives and beetroot julienne. Serve at once.

Wine advice: because of the thyme, choose a spiced Gewurztraminer.

Red mullet fillets, tuna fish brandade

RECIPE PAGE 78

Brandade is usually made with salt cod, but I love this tuna version served with red mullet.

Red mullet fillets, tuna fish brandade

Difficulty: ♜♜

Preparation: 20 mn

Cooking time: 1 h 30

Ingredients for four people

1 tuna fish (about 1 kg)
4 large potatoes (Rattes du Touquet)
100 g butter
1 bunch of chives
8 red mullet fillets (about 80 g each)

Salt
Freshly-ground pepper

Tuna fish consommé
1 carrot
2 onions
1 head of garlic
1/2 bunch dill
3 juniper berries
1 clove
1 *bouquet garni**
200 g butter

Prepare tuna fish consommé: fillet the tuna and remove the bones. Set aside. Peel the carrot and onions and cut into large pieces. Put the tuna's head and bone, vegetables, garlic, dill, juniper, clove and *bouquet garni** in a large pot and immerse in water to about 2 in above the surface. Reduce by three quarters on high heat. Strain. Before serving, add 100 g butter and reduce by three quarters. Keep warm.

Prepare tuna fish brandade: dice tuna fillets. Set aside. Preheat the oven to 400 °F (200 °C, gas mark 6) and bake the unpeeled potatoes for 30 minutes. Peel and mash the potatoes in a bowl with a fork. Add the butter, chopped chives and diced tuna fish. Keep warm.

When serving: place 1 or 2 spoonfuls of tuna and potato mixture on each soup plate. Add the red mullet fillets. Preheat the oven to 400 °F (200 °C, gas mark 6) and cook for 3 minutes. Coat with the tuna consommé. Serve at once.

Wine advice: with such mixed flavors, red mullet and tuna fish, choose a sunny red wine, a Palette, from the Aix-en-Provence region.

Red mullet with cream of broad beans

Difficulty: 2

Preparation: 20 mn

Cooking time: 50 mn

Ingredients for four people

8 fillets of red mullet (about 100 g each)

Cream of broad beans
1 onion
1 carrot
1 clove of garlic
200 g butter
80 g smoked bacon
100 g shelled broad beans
200 g shelled peas
1 *bouquet garni**
1 l chicken stock*
3 tablespoons double cream

Salt
Freshly-ground pepper

Prepare cream of broad beans: peel and chop up the onion. Peel and slice the carrot. Peel the garlic. Heat 50 g butter in a saucepan. Sauté the vegetables and bacon for few minutes. Add the broad beans, peas and the *bouquet garni**. Pour on the chicken stock* and allow to simmer for 45 minutes. Remove the *bouquet garni** and blend. Reduce by half. Add the cream and the remaining butter. Mix well and keep warm.

Prepare red mullets: peel 2 fillets with great care and keep the skins. Remove the bones. Place the fillets at right angles on one skin and roll up. Do the same with the 6 remaining fillets. Preheat the oven to 400 °F (200 °C, gas mark 6) and bake for 5 minutes.

When serving: place some cream on each soup plate and top with the red mullet fillets. Serve hot.

Wine advice: choose a Saint-Joseph, a white Côtes du Rhône which will suit this dish perfectly.

Skate winglets, lettuce with dried fruit spread

RECIPE PAGE 84

Romaine lettuce is a delightful combination with skate, with mushrooms to blend the flavors.

Skate winglets, lettuce with dried fruit spread

Difficulty: ♜♜

Preparation: 10 mn

Cooking time: 20 mn

Ingredients for four people

4 skate winglets (about 150 g each)
1/4 bunch chives

Mushroom butter
200 g mushrooms
300 g butter
4 tablespoons capers
1/4 bunch chives
1/4 bunch chervil
3 leaves of basil
3 sprigs of coriander

Salt
Freshly-ground pepper

Lettuce with dried fruit spread
1 romaine lettuce
80 g hazelnuts
80 g almonds
80 g pistachio
80 g walnuts
1 tablespoon oil
100 g butter

Lemon butter
200 g butter
Juice of 2 lemons

Prepare mushroom butter: clean and dice them. Heat 150 g butter in a skillet. Add mushrooms, cover and cook for 5 minutes on a low heat. Remove from the heat and add the drained capers and the chopped herbs. Mix and set aside.

Prepare romaine lettuce: wash the lettuce and set aside 4 leaves (not too green). Shred the remaining lettuce. Pan-fry the dried fruit with oil. Set aside. Gently cook the shredded lettuce with butter. Add the dried fruit and keep warm.

Prepare skate winglets: heat 150 g butter in a skillet. Cook the skate for 2 minutes on both sides. Put them on an oven tray and spread on the mushroom butter. Preheat the oven grill. Place the skate under the grill for 5 minutes.

Prepare the lemon butter: melt the butter with the lemon juice. Season and keep warm.

When serving: spread the romaine and fruit mixture on each lettuce leaf. Place a skate winglet on each plate. Top with the stuffed lettuce and pour on a spoonful of lemon butter. Serve hot.

Wine advice: choose a full-bodied white wine, such as a Chassagne-Montrachet *1er Cru*.

John Dory, vermicelli and lamb sauce

Ingredients for four people

Difficulty:

Preparation: 10 mn

Cooking time: 15 mn

4 John Dory fillets (about 150 g each)
1/2 l lamb stock*
250 g butter
1/2 bunch chervil
1/4 bunch coriander
4 large tomatoes
8 tablespoons vermicelli
2 tablespoons oil

Salt
Freshly-ground pepper

Prepare the sauce: pour the lamb stock* into a saucepan. Add 200 g butter. Reduce by three quarters. Keep warm. Set aside. Remove the leaves from the chervil and coriander. Scald the tomatoes, then peel them and remove the seeds and cut them into large pieces. Set aside.

Before serving: cook vermicelli in 1/2 l salted water for 3 minutes. Meanwhile, heat the butter and oil on high heat. Cook John Dory fillets for 2 minutes on both sides. Drain the vermicelli.

When serving: place 2 spoonfuls of vermicelli on each plate. Add the John Dory fillet and place the tomatoes around it. Coat with the lamb sauce. Sprinkle on the herbs. Serve hot.

Wine advice: with this fine fish, choose a subtle, mild wine like a Pouilly-Fumé, if possible 1995, a particulary good vintage.

Hake matelote and artichoke ravioli

RECIPE PAGE 88

Artichoke and hake: two tastes of Brittany, combined with a sauce from Alsace.

Hake matelote and artichoke ravioli

Difficulty: 2

Preparation: 15 mn

Cooking time: 1 h

Ingredients for four people

1 hake (about 2 kg)
4 large artichokes
100 g butter
4 tablespoons veal stock*
3 basil leaves
6 tablespoons double cream
4 squares of Chinese ravioli dough (9 cm sides)

Salt
Freshly-ground pepper

Hake stock
1/2 l dry white wine
1 *bouquet garni**
1 onion
2 shallots
1 clove
3 juniper berries

Prepare hake stock: wash and gut the fish. Remove the head and tail. Cut into 4 large pieces and remove the bones. Put the head, tail and bones in a large saucepan. Cover with the wine and 1/2 l water. Add the *bouquet garni**, chopped onion and shallots, the clove and juniper berries. Reduce by three quarters. Strain. Set aside.

Prepare artichoke: remove leaves and base. Finely mince the artichoke hearts. Cook them gently in the butter for 15 minutes with veal stock*. Remove from heat and add the chopped basil. Set aside.

Prepare the hake: place the pieces of hake on an ovenproof dish and pour on the hake stock. Preheat the oven to 460 °F (240 °C, gas mark 8). Bake for 25 minutes. Remove the fish and strain the stock. Add the double cream and cook for 10 minutes. Set aside.

When serving: fry the squares of Chinese ravioli in a deep-fryer. Place some sliced artichoke and the hake on each plate. Pour on some stock and top with the ravioli. Serve at once.

Wine advice: choose a white Croze-Hermitage, a wine from the Rhône valley.

Tuna fish tournedos with girolles and creamy spelt

Ingredients for four people

Difficulty :

Preparation : 10 mn

Cooking time : 15 mn

4 white tuna fish steaks (about 150 g each)
1/2 l beef stock*
350 g spelt
350 g butter
100 g mascarpone
1 kg girolles
4 tablespoons olive oil
1/2 bunch chives
2 bunches curly parsley

Salt
Freshly-ground pepper

Prepare creamy spelt : boil the beef stock* in a large saucepan, add the spelt. Cook and stir for 10 minutes. Fold in 100 g butter and mascarpone. Keep warm.

Prepare the girolles : wash carefully and fry them in the olive oil, just to evaporate the water. Drain. Heat 100 g butter in the skillet and brown the mushrooms for 2 minutes. Season and add the chopped chives. Set aside. Fry the parsley in a deep-fryer. Keep warm.

Prepare tuna fish : heat 150 g butter in a skillet and sauté the tuna steaks for 3 minutes on each side.

When serving : pour a large spoonful of creamy spelt on each plate. Arrange the sautéed tuna and the girolles around it. Sprinkle on the fried parsley. Serve hot.

Wine advice : for this rich, savory dish, choose a white wine from Côte de Beaune, a Meursault or a Puligny-Montrachet.

Red mullet, candied lemon and vegetable cake

RECIPE PAGE 92

Moroccon - style lemons and citrus-flavored vegetables complement the mullet.

Red mullet, candied lemon and vegetable cake

Difficulty: A A A

Preparation: 20 mn

Cooking time: 1 h 45

Standing time: 4 h

Ingredients for four people

8 red mullet fillets (about 100g each)

Stewed candied lemons
4 lemons
200 g caster sugar
Juice of 4 lemons
1 mango

Balsamic vinegar vinaigrette
2 teaspoons balsamic vinegar
3 tablespoons olive oil
Juice of 1/2 orange
1 candied lemon
2 slices of fresh ginger

Salt
Freshly-ground pepper

4 individual tins (10 cm in diameter)

Vegetable cakes
1 large onion
1 large carrot
1 fennel head
1 tablespoon raisins
1 tablespoon almonds
4 dried apricots
1 candied lemon
5 mint leaves
10 coriander leaves
2 tablespoons olive oil
10 g powdered ginger
4 sheets of phyllo pastry
50 g butter
1 teaspoon caster sugar

Prepare stewed lemons: peel the lemons and cut them into a *brunoise*. Blanch three times. Weigh them and place in a saucepan. Add the same weight of water and caster sugar. Cook gently for 1 hour and a half, until you obtain a purée. Meanwhile, reduce the lemon juice by three quarters and set aside. Peel and dice the mango and dry it on a high heat. Blend. Mix the stewed lemons, juices and puréed mango. Set aside in the refrigerator for at least 4 hours.

Prepare balsamic vinegar vinaigrette: cut the candied lemon and ginger into a *brunoise*. Mix the vinegar and oil in a blender. Add the orange juice, the candied lemon and the ginger. Season. Blend again. Set aside.

Prepare vegetable cakes: peel the onion, carrot and fennel. Cut them and the dried fruit into a *mirepoix*. Chop the mint and the coriander. Heat the olive oil and ginger and cook all the fruit and vegetables gently for 1 hour and half, until you obtain a candied mixture. Cut the sheets of phyllo pastry into 8 squares of 24 cm sides. Butter the molds. Line an individual tin with the first phyllo sheet. Butter a second phyllo sheet, line and fill with vegetables and fold down the edges. Do the same for the three other cakes. Preheat the oven to 350 °F (180 °C, gas mark 5) and bake for 10 minutes. Turn over the cakes and sprinkle with caster sugar. Brown them under the oven grill for a few moments. Keep warm.

Prepare the red mullet fillets: peel 2 fillets with great care. Remove the bones. Place the fillets at right angles on one skin and roll up. Do the same with the 6 remaining fillets. Preheat the oven to 400 °F (200 °C, gas mark 6) and bake for 5 minutes.

When serving: set one vegetable cake on each plate. Add the red mullet fillets. Place a quenelle of stewed candied lemons on top and a dash of balsamic vinaigrette.

Wine advise: choose a tangy wine: a Jurançon, because of its candied lemon flavor, a wine from the Pau region.

Bass in tinfoil with citrus fruit sauce and braised lettuce

RECIPE PAGE 96

The braised lettuce is a delicate match for the king of fishes: the bass.

Bass in tinfoil with citrus fruit sauce and braised lettuce

Difficulty: ♜♜

Preparation: 15 mn

Cooking time: 1 h 10

INGREDIENTS FOR FOUR PEOPLE

4 thick bass steaks, with skin (about 160 g each)
2 lettuces
100 g butter
2 onions
2 carrots
1/4 l veal stock*
4 large spinach leaves

CITRUS FRUIT SAUCE
1/2 l mussel gravy*
Juice of 2 oranges
Juice of 1 lemon
Juice of 1 grapefruit
150 g butter

Salt
Freshly-ground pepper

Tinfoil

Prepare braised lettuces: wash and blanch the lettuces and dip them in cold water. Drain and press. Cut the lettuces in half and remove the hearts. Heat the butter in a pan and brown the chopped onions and the *brunoise* of carrots. Add the lettuces and cover with the veal stock*. Preheat the oven to 250 °F (120 °C, gas mark 3) and bake for 45 minutes. Meanwhile, blanch the spinach leaves. Drain the lettuces, strain the vegetable cooking juice and set aside. Set a half lettuce on each spinach leaf and add a spoonful of vegetables. Fold into a tube. Set aside.

Prepare the citrus fruit sauce: pour the mussel gravy* and fruit juices into a saucepan. Add the butter and reduce by three quarters on a high heat. Season. Set aside.

Prepare the bass in tinfoil: cut four 20 cm squares in the tinfoil. Place one piece of bass on each. Pour on a spoonful of citrus fruit sauce and fold the foil in two. Preheat the oven to 460 °F (240 °C, gas mark 8) and bake for 15 minutes. Meanwhile, strain the citrus fruit juice and emulsify it.

When serving: place a piece of bass and a braised lettuce on each plate and coat with fruit juice. Serve hot.

Wine advice: a white Marsannay, a fine, elegant wine would be a good choice for this simple recipe.

Fillet of turbot and bacon risotto

INGREDIENTS FOR FOUR PEOPLE — Difficulty: 2

4 turbot steaks (about 400 g each)
8 tablespoons olive oil
150 g bacon
150 g smoked bacon
50 g butter
250 g *langoustine* stock*

BACON RISOTTO
1 large onion
60 g butter
380 g Arborio rice
3/4 l chicken stock*
4 tablespoons of mascarpone
1 bunch chives

Salt
Freshly-ground pepper

Preparation: 20 mn

Cooking time: 25 mn

Prepare turbot: heat 6 tablespoons olive oil in a skillet. Sauté turbot fillets for 2 minutes on each side. Preheat the oven to 420 °F (210 °C, gas mark 7). Place the fish on an oven tray and bake for 5 minutes. Remove the bones and set aside.

Prepare the bacon risotto: peel and chop the onion. Cook the butter, the rice and half of chicken stock*. Cook on a medium heat stirring continuously. After 3/4 cooking time, pour in the remaining stock. Cook and stir until all the stock is absorbed. Remove from the heat and add the mascarpone and chopped chive. Keep warm.

Before serving: sauté the diced bacon. Drain and set aside.

When serving: place the risotto and bacon on each plate and top gently with the turbot. Coat with the *langoustine* stock*. Serve hot.

Wine advice: choose a great Burgundy white wine, maybe a Corton-Charlemagne, vintage 1990.

3

meat

Boiled pigeon with baby vegetables and foie gras

RECIPE PAGE **102**

A boiled free-range Vendée pigeon with baby vegetables and slices of *foie gras* to thicken the consommé.

Boiled pigeon with baby vegetables and foie gras

Difficulty: ♜♜♜

Preparation: 30 mn

Cooking time: 2 h 30

Ingredients for four people

2 good-sized Vendée pigeons
2 carrots
1 large leek
2 onions
1 turnip
1 stick of celery
1 *bouquet garni**
1 head of garlic
1 kg chuck beef
1 calf's foot
100 g sausage meat
100 g caul casing
4 *foie gras* escalopes (90 g each)

Salt
Coarse salt
Freshly- ground pepper

Young vegetables
500 g garden peas
1 kg broad beans
16 spring onions
12 mini-carrots
12 mini-turnips
12 mini-leeks

Prepare pigeons: bone the pigeons or ask your poultry dealer to do it. Set aside the giblets and carcass.

Prepare the boiled meat with vegetables: wash the vegetables and cut them into large pieces. Put the chuck beef, calf's foot, carcass, vegetables and salt into a large pot. Add water until 5 cm covers the ingredients. Boil and skim. Cook gently for 2 hours. Remove meat. Strain and set aside the consommé. Clarify the consommé until you obtain about 1 l.

Stuff pigeons' legs: wash the caul casing, dry and lay it on the table. Check that the legs are completely boned. Line each pigeon leg with sausage meat. Cut the caul casing into 4 pieces. Roll up the caul casing into a small *gigot* shape.

Prepare young vegetables: shell the garden peas, wash the broad beans, peel the onions, mini-carrots, mini-turnips and mini-leeks. In a large saucepan, boil all the vegetables for 3 minutes in salted water. Drain and leave to cool. Set aside.

Before serving: place the pigeon legs in 1/2 l clarified consommé. Cook for 10 mn. Add the fillets and cook for a further 3 minutes. Remove the fillets. Add the remaining consommé and mix gently. Keep warm.

When serving: fry the *foie gras* escalopes for 3 minutes on each side, in a skillet, on a high heat. Place the fillets, legs and *foie gras* on 4 soup plates. Add the vegetables. Pour on a ladle of warm consommé. Serve at once.

Wine advice: choose a full-bodied wine, such as a Pomerol or a Saint-Julien.

Knuckle of veal, langoustines and candied lemon sauce

RECIPE PAGE 106

Why not bring together two creatures who never meet? I can assure you, they complement each other very well.

Knuckle of veal, langoustines and candied lemon sauce

Difficulty: AAA

Preparation: 20 mn

Cooking time: 3 h

INGREDIENTS FOR FOUR PEOPLE

2 knuckles of veal, with bones
1 stalk of celery
2 leeks
2 onions
1 carrot
1 head of garlic
2 teaspoons powdered curry
2 sprigs of thyme
2 bay leaves
1 candied lemon
1/2 l veal stock*
12 *langoustines*
1 tablespoon oil olive

VEGETABLE *MIREPOIX*
100 g carrots
100 g leeks
100 g celery
200 g chard ribs
1 candied lemon
100 g onions
150g butter

Salt
Freshly-ground pepper

4 skewers

Prepare knuckles of veal: peel the celery, leeks, onions and carrot and cut them into large pieces. Crush the head of garlic. Place the vegetables in a large cast-iron stewpan, add the curry, thyme and bay leaves. Add the quartered lemon and pour in the veal stock*. Put the knuckles in the stewpan and season. Preheat the oven to 400 °F (200 °C, gas mark 6). Bake for 3 hours. When knuckles are cooked, set them aside and keep warm. Strain the stock and reduce by three quarters.

Prepare vegetable *mirepoix*: peel the vegetables and cut them into a *mirepoix*. Heat the butter in a stewpan. Add the carrots and 4 minutes later, all the other vegetables. Cook for 10 minutes. Set aside.

Before serving: shell the *langoustines* and keep the tails only. Sauté the *langoustines* for 2 minutes on both sides. Put 3 *langoustines* on each skewer. Season and set aside.

When serving: slice the knuckles into large escalopes. Place the *mirepoix*, on each plate, with a slice of meat and a skewer, as you can see on page 105. Coat with the reduced sauce. Serve hot.

Wine advice: serve with a Burgundy wine from Côte de Beaune, such as a Santenay or a Côte chalonnaise or a Mercurey.

Saddle of rabbit with bone marrow ravioli

Ingredients for four people — Difficulty: ♜♜♜

Preparation: 30 mn

Cooking time: 30 mn

2 rabbits
2 carrots
2 onions
1 leek
1 l dry white wine
1/4 l chicken stock*
1 *bouquet garni**
250 g butter
2 tablespoons breadcrumbs
Salt
Freshly-ground pepper

Bone marrow ravioli
200 g bone marrow (without the bone)
30 g shallots
20 g flat leaf parsley
1 egg
80 g breadcrumbs
1 pinch of nutmeg
10 g flour
8 pieces of Chinese ravioli dough
1 egg yolk

Prepare bone marrow ravioli: force the marrow through a fine mesh sieve and set aside in a salad bowl. Peel and finely chop the shallots. Put them in the salad bowl and add the egg, breadcrumbs, parsley, nutmeg and flour. Mix well. Brush the sides of the dough pieces with the beaten egg yolk. Place some stuffing in the center of each. Close and seal the edges. Boil some salted water in a large saucepan and poach the ravioli for 2 minutes. Drain on muslin. Set aside.

Prepare the rabbit stock: cut the rabbits into pieces, but keep the legs and saddles whole. Peel and cut the vegetables into large pieces. Pour the dry white wine and the chicken stock* into a large pot. Add the vegetables, *bouquet garni** and rabbit pieces. Cook for 15 minutes. Remove the rabbit pieces and reduce by three quarters. Strain. Add 150 g butter and reduce again by half. Season and set aside.

Before serving: bone the rabbit legs and saddles and reshape them. Breadcrumb each piece. Heat 100 g butter in a skillet and fry the rabbit pieces for 5 to 6 minutes.

When serving: place a leg, a saddle and one ravioli on each plate. Coat them with the rabbit stock. Serve at once.

Wine advice: choose a Burgundy wine, not too full-bodied: a Volnay or a Chassagne-Montrachet.

Chicken, olive sauce and crushed potatoes

Difficulty: 2/3

Preparation: 20 mn

Cooking time: 1 h 30

Ingredients for four people

1 Bresse chicken (about 2,2 kg)
150 g sausage meat
5 basil leaves
5 shallots
1 *bouquet garni**
1 head of garlic
50 g butter
1 tablespoon peanut oil
1 l of chicken stock*

Salt
Freshly-ground pepper

Olive sauce
200 g black olives from Nice
100 g green olives in brine
50 g butter

Crushed potatoes
5 large Roseval potatoes
100 g butter

Clingfilm
Tinfoil

Prepare the chicken: bone the legs and keep the bones. Cut each leg into two pieces. Prepare the stuffing: dice the liver and mix with the sausage meat and chopped basil. Mix well. Lay clingfilm about 24 x 24 cm square on your work surface, flatten a 1/2 chicken leg and spread with stuffing. Roll tightly and close the film to obtain a large sausage shape. Do the same for the other 1/2 legs. Set aside the chicken fillets. Keep the carcass. Peel and chop the shallots and garlic. Heat the butter and oil in a large saucepan. Brown the shallots and garlic and add the carcass, the *bouquet garni** and chicken stock*. Add the stuffed legs and cook for 1 hour on a medium heat. Carefully remove the legs and add the chicken fillets. Cook for 7 minutes. Remove the fillets and keep them warm. Keep the cooking juice.

Prepare the olive juice: pour the chicken gravy into a saucepan. Add the black olives and green olives in brine. Reduce by three quarters. Fold in 50 g butter and whisk until you obtain a creamy sauce.

Prepare crushed potatoes: wrap each potato in the tin foil. Preheat the oven to 400 °F (200 °C, gas mark 6). Bake the potatoes for 1 hour. When they are cooked, scoop out four of them. Mash with 100 g butter. Season. Peel the fifth and finely slice it. Fry in a deep-fryer. Drain on a paper towel.

When serving: arrange three spoonfuls of potatoes and chips on each plate. Slice one leg and one breast of the chicken and place over the potatoes. Coat with the olive sauce. Serve hot.

Wine advice: choose a Chambolle-Musigny, a very light Burgundy wine from Côte de Nuits which goes well with this Bresse chicken.

Roast duckling, fresh cream cheese *quenelles*

RECIPE PAGE **112**

Discover several French regions in one recipe with a roast duckling from Vendée, fresh cream cheese *quenelles* from Alsace and Mediterranean olives and tomatoes.

Roast duckling, fromage frais quenelles

Difficulty : ♦♦

Preparation : 15 mn

Standing time : 3 h

Cooking time : 1 h

Ingredients for four people

2 ducklings
1 l veal stock*
100 g black olives from Nice
1 stalk citronella
3 cl green olives in brine
1/2 preserved lemon
4 preserved tomatoes*

Piping bag

FRESH CREAM CHEESE *QUENELLES*
250 g fromage frais
3 eggs
125 g flour
1 pinch nutmeg
30 g butter

Salt
Freshly-ground pepper

Prepare *quenelles* : whisk the *fromage frais* with the eggs. Add the flour, nutmeg and softened butter. Mix well. Season. Set aside for 3 hours before use. Pour the mixture into the unribbed pastry tube and make 12 *quenelles*. Drop them into a pan of boiling salted water. Remove them gently with a slotted spoon when they rise to the surface. Drain on a paper towel. Set aside.

Prepare duckling : ask your poultry dealer to gut and dress the ducklings. Put them on an oven tray with the veal stock*. Preheat the oven to 460 °F (240 °C, gas mark 8). Bake the ducklings for 45 mn. Remove from the oven.

Prepare the sauce : strain the cooking gravy and pour into a saucepan. Add the olives in brine, diced lemon and black olives. Cook gently for 10 minutes. Carve the ducklings. Chop the citronella. Set aside.

When serving : place one leg and one wing on each plate. Add 3 *quenelles*, a preserved tomato* and coat with duckling sauce. Sprinkle on chopped citronella. Serve hot.

Wine advice : a Saint-Émilion will be the perfect match for this duckling.

Beef fillet, red wine sauce and kromesky fritters

Ingredients for four people

Difficulty: (2)

Preparation: 10 mn

Cooking time: 1 h 10

4 beef fillet steaks, about 150 g each
50 g butter
40 cl red wine sauce with shallots*
1 handful curled endive
1 tablespoon olive oil

Kromesky fritters
6 large Roseval potatoes
100 g diced bacon
150g butter
100 g grated Parmesan cheese

Breadcrumb coating
300 g breadcrumbs
3 eggs
4 tablespoons flour
1/2 l milk

Salt
Freshly-ground pepper

Kitchen paper

Prepare kromesky fritters: preheat the oven to 400 °F (200 °C, gas mark 6) and bake the unpeeled potatoes for 1 hour. Brown the diced bacon in a skillet on a high heat. Set aside. Remove the potatoes from the oven and core them. Mash the flesh with a fork. Add the butter, diced bacon and Parmesan cheese. Use two tablespoons to shape the mixture into 12 egg-shaped *quenelles*. Set aside.

Prepare breadcrumb coating: whisk the breadcrumbs, eggs, flour and milk in a bowl. Coat the fritters. Heat the oil in a deep fryer. Cook for about 4 minutes. Drain on a kitchen paper. Keep warm.

When serving: cook the beef fillets in a skillet on a high heat, according to taste. Place one on each plate. Top with 3 kromesky fritters. Add some curled endive. Pour on the red wine sauce with shallots*. Serve at once.

Wine advice: choose a great Médoc, such as Pauillac or Margaux.

Veal entrecote with preserved vegetables

Difficulty: ♜

Preparation: 10 mn

Cooking time: 30 mn

INGREDIENTS FOR FOUR PEOPLE

4 boned veal rib steaks
1 l chicken stock*
1 head of celeriac
4 carrots
3 heads of garlic
16 pearl onions
1 kg broad beans
10 cl double cream
20 g butter
2 tablespoons oil

Salt
Freshly-ground pepper

Prepare preserved vegetables: peel the celeriac and carrots. Cut them into sticks about 7 cm long by 1 cm wide. Shell the broad beans, peel the onions and garlic. Cook the chicken stock* and carrots for 8 minutes into a saucepan. Add the celeriac, broad beans, garlic and onions. Cook for a further 10 minutes. Remove the vegetables from the stock and keep them warm. Strain the stock and fold in the double cream. Reduce by three quarters. Keep warm.

Prepare veal entrecotes: heat the mixture of butter and oil in a skillet. Cook the entrecotes for 4 minutes on both sides.

When serving: place a ribsteak on each plate, surrounded by the vegetables. Coat with the reduced sauce. Serve at once.

Wine advice: you may choose a Burgundy wine for this white meat recipe. Perhaps a Mercurey, or, why not, a Julienas, a wine from the northern Beaujolais.

Veal sweetbreads, morel mushrooms and asparagus

Difficulty: 2/2

Preparation: 10 mn

Cooking time: 50 mn

Ingredients for four people

4 good-sized veal sweetbreads
20 green asparagus
3/4 l chicken stock*
400 g fresh morel mushrooms
150 g butter
4 tablespoons truffle juice

Aromatic stock for sweetbreads
1 leek
1 carrot
1 tablespoon flour
Juice of 1 lemon
1 *bouquet garni**

Salt
Freshly-ground pepper

Blanch the sweetbreads: peel and dice the leek and carrot into large pieces. Boil 1 l salted water in a large saucepan. Add the flour, lemon juice, leek, carrot and the *bouquet garni**. Cook for 30 minutes. Remove the fine-skin from the sweetbreads and add them to the stock. Cook for 10 minutes and remove at once. Drain and set aside.

Prepare the asparagus: peel the asparagus. Boil the chicken stock* in a large pot and add the asparagus. Cook on a medium heat for about 7 minutes. Drain and set aside. Boil fresh morel mushrooms for 2 minutes. Drain. Reduce the stock by three quarters. Fold in 50 g butter and stir until smooth. Add the truffle juice. Keep warm.

Before serving: heat 100 g butter in a skillet. Sauté the sweetbreads for 10 minutes.

When serving: lay 5 asparagus on each plate, add the morel mushrooms and sautéed sweetbreads. Coat with sauce. Serve warm.

Wine advice: this rich and savory dish deserves an amber-yellow wine from the Jura, vintage 1988.

4

desserts

Pajaro strawberries carpaccio with five sugars

RECIPE PAGE 122

This dessert is not only attractive but easy to do, and if you use the right sugars, it's absolutly magic !

Pajaro strawberries carpaccio with five sugars

Difficulty :

Preparation : 10 mn

INGREDIENTS FOR FOUR PEOPLE

1 kg Pajaro strawberries
100 g caster sugar
1 teaspoon powdered cinnamon
100 g Muscovado cane sugar
1 teaspoon powdered ginger
100 g Demerara sugar
Zest of 1 lemon
100 g Dark Muscovado sugar
SZest of 1 orange
100 g molasses
1/2 nutmeg

5 small dishes

Prepare the five sugars : in the first small dish, mix the caster sugar with the cinnamon. In the second, mix the Muscovado cane sugar with ginger. In the third, finely grate the peel of the lemon. Mix the zest with the Demerara sugar. In the fourth, finely grate the peel of the orange. Mix the zest with Dark Muscovado sugar. In the fifth, mix molasses and the 1/2 grated nutmeg.

Prepare the strawberries : it is not necessary to wash strawberries, simply roll them gently in a damp cloth. Remove the stalks, slice the fruit and place them on a serving dish. Serve with the five small dishes of sugar.

Wine advice : this simple dessert goes well with a dainty, elegant wine, with a taste of candied fruits : the Bonnezeaux, from the Loire region.

Gingerbread and caramelized apples

Difficulty: ▲▲▲

Preparation: 25 mn

Cooking time: 1 h 10

Ice maker: 30 mn

Ingredients for four people

Gingerbread
150 g honey
7 g ginger spice
150 g flour
3 g bicarbonate of soda
2 g baking powder
125 g milk
6 eggs
140 g butter
50 g orange marmalade
150 g sugar

Rectangular cake tin
Greaseproof paper
Ice-maker

Vanilla ice cream
2 vanilla pods
450 g milk
100 g single cream
8 egg yolks
125 g sugar

Caramelized apples
6 Canada apples
80 g sugar
100 g butter
1 pinch powdered cinnamon
50 g redcurrant jelly
50 g water

Prepare gingerbread: preheat the oven to 310 F° (160 C°, gas mark 4). Cook the honey and spices in a pan on a low heat. In a bowl, mix the flour with the bicarbonate of soda and baking powder. In another one, mix 100 g milk with 3 eggs and add the warm honey. Mix gently. Add the flour mixture, and then the melted butter and the orange marmalade. Line a cake tin with greaseproof paper, pour in the mixture and bake for 35 minutes. Allow to cool.

Prepare vanilla ice: in a pan, boil the milk, single cream and the vanilla pods split and scraped. In a bowl, mix the sugar with the egg yolks until the mixture becomes frothy. Remove the milk from the heat and add the eggs. Strain. Cook over a medium heat, stirring with a wooden spoon until it is coated by the liquid. Allow to cool. Pour it into the ice-maker. Then set aside in a refrigerator.

Prepare the caramelized apples: peel and core the apples. Put them on an ovenproof dish and put the sugar, butter, cinnamon and redcurrant jelly on each apple. Pour the water around them. Preheat the oven to 400°F (200°C, gas mark 6) and bake for 30 minutes. Set aside and keep warm.

When serving: break 3 whole eggs into a dish and whisk them. Pour 25 g milk into another dish. Cut the gingerbread into slices. Dip 4 slices first in the milk and then in the eggs. Heat 100 g butter in a skillet. Pan-fry the gingerbread slices rapidly until they turn pale yellow. On each serving plate, place one slice of bread, a caramelized apple and a bowl of vanilla ice.

Wine advice : simply choose a very good cider.

Menton lemon soufflé and citrus fruit

RECIPE PAGE 128

A soufflé isn't easy to do, especially four individual ones! However, don't panic, just follow the recipe and don't burn your fingers!

Menton lemon soufflé and citrus fruit

Difficulty: ♜♜♜

Preparation: 20 mn

Cooking time: 45 mn

Ingredients for four people

LEMON SOUFFLÉ
Zest of 1 lemon
150g Menton lemon juice
1 vanilla pod
140 g powdered sugar
12 g flour
6 g cornstarch
50 g milk
11 egg yolks
6 egg whites
50 g butter
1 tablespoon icing sugar

STEWED CITRUS FRUITS
1/2 grapefruit
2 oranges
1 lemon
65 g granulated sugar
1/2 l water

4 individual moulds

Prepare stewed citrus fruit: scald the fruit whole, drain and cut into small pieces. Heat the sugar in a saucepan until you obtain a dry caramel. Add the fruit and water. Cook slowly until you obtain a compote.

Prepare soufflé: finely grate the peel of the lemon. Boil the lemon juice, the zest and the split vanilla pod. In the meantime, mix 75 g sugar, flour, cornstarch and milk in a bowl. With a whisk, fold in the 10 egg yolks one by one. Pour the mixture into the lemon juice, and cook over a medium heat, while stirring with the whisk, until you obtain a smooth cream. It can be prepared to this point then transferred to the bain-marie.

When serving: beat the egg whites with 65 g sugar until you obtain a frothy mixture. Add one egg yolk to the mixture in the bain-marie, and then fold in the whites. Mix gently. Butter the moulds, sprinkle on icing sugar and pour one tablespoon of stewed fruit into each. Add the soufflé mixture. Preheat the oven to 350 °F (180 °C, gas mark 5). Bake for 12 minutes. Serve at once.

Wine advice: a Jurançon wine blends well with the citrus fruit aroma.

Brioche tartlets, cinnamon pears and savoury caramel

INGREDIENTS FOR FOUR PEOPLE

Difficulté :

BRIOCHE TARTLETS
125 g brioche pastry dough*
25 g butter
125 g fresh cream cheese
20 g caster sugar
1/2 egg
25 g powdered cinnamon
1 cinnamon stick

4 individual tartlet tins

SAVOURY CARAMEL
100 g caster sugar
55 g single cream
1 g salt from Guérande
37 g butter
15 g white fondant

CINNAMON PEARS
4 Comice pears
1 lemon juice
260 g caster sugar
1 cinnamon stick
25 g butter

Préparation : 20 mn

Cooking time : 15 mn

Prepare tartlets : divide the brioche pastry dough* into 4 equal portions. Arrange the portions in buttered tartlet tins and set aside, in a cool place, to rise, for 1 hour. In a bowl, whisk the fresh cream cheese, sugar and 1/2 egg. Set aside in the refrigerator.

Prepare salted caramel : dry cook the sugar slowly in a pan until you obtain a golden caramel. Add the lukewarm single cream and the Guérande salt. Allow to cool. Pour into a mixer and fold in the butter and the fondant. Mix until you obtain a smooth, creamy caramel.

Prepare cinnamon pears : peel the pears, cut them into two pieces and remove cores. Gently mix them with the juice of 1 lemon. Set aside. Make a syrup with 1/2 l water, 250 g sugar and cinnamon. Add the pears and simmer until soft (test with a knife blade). In a skillet, brown 10 g sugar. Add 25 g butter and roast the pears on all sides until a rich golden color.

When serving : fill the tartlets with the caramel and then with the fresh cream cheese. Sprinkle with powdered cinnamon. Preheat the oven to 25 F° (220 C°, gas mark 7) and bake for 5 minutes. Put one tartlet and pear on each plate and decorate with cinnamon sticks cut lenghtwise. Serve hot.

Wine advice : to bring out the caramel and vanilla flavours, choose a white Banyuls wine.

Soft lime macaroons, red fruit sauce

RECIPE PAGE 132

If you cannot find raspberries of a high enough quality, use another red soft fruit such as strawberries, mulberries or redcurrants.

Soft lime macaroons, red fruit sauce

Difficulty: ♜♜♜

Preparation: 30 mn

Cooking time: 20 mn

Ingredients for four people

4 punnets of raspberries
100 g dry nougatine *
30 g thinly-shredded lime zest

Macaroons
150 g icing sugar
100 g ground almonds
Zest of 1 lime
3 egg whites
50 g caster sugar

Greaseproof paper
Piping bag

Lemon curd filling
185 g lemon juice
5 eggs
100 g sugar
Zest of 2 lemons
125 g butter

Wild strawberries sauce
125 g wild strawberries
50 g sugar
Juice of 2 lemons
50 g Mara wild strawberries

Prepare macaroons: preheat the oven to 300 °F (150 °C, gas mark 4). In a bowl, mix icing sugar, ground almonds and thinly-shredded lime zest. Beat the egg whites with the caster sugar until they are firm. Fold the whites into the almond mixture. Stir gently with a spatula. Line a baking tray with greaseproof paper, then pipe dollops of the mixture on it. Bake for 10 to 12 minutes. The outside should be crisp and the inside soft. Remove from the oven, pour a little water between the paper and the baking tray: this makes it easier to separate the macaroons, and preserve their softness. Set aside.

Prepare lemon filling: mix all the ingredients except for the butter in a saucepan, and cook slowly, stirring until you obtain a creamy mixture. Take the pan off the heat and add the butter. Mix. Set aside in the refrigerator.

Prepare the sauce: mix all the ingredients in a blender. Strain. Set aside.

When serving: place a dessert spoon of lemon curd on the flat side of the macaroon and cover with another macaroon. Arrange the macaroons and raspberries on each plate as in the picture, p.131. Pour over some sauce, dredge dry nougatine* and decorate with the lemon julienne.

Wine advice: simply pink Champagne.

Picnic cake with ginger and orange

Ingredients for four people

Difficulty: ♜♜

Preparation: 20 mn

Cooking time: 40 mn

Ginger cake
Zest of 1 orange
50 g fresh grated ginger
250 g butter
250 g caster sugar
5 eggs
250 g flour
50 g cristallized ginger
8 candied orange slices

Cake tin (20 cm)

Orange marmalade
5 oranges
100 g caster sugar
50 g butter
100 g water
Juice of 1 lemon

Strussel
100 g butter
100 g caster sugar
100 g ground almonds
100 g flour

Prepare the picnic cake: preheat the oven to 350 °F (180 °C, gas mark 5). Use a fine grater to obtain the orange zest. Set aside. Dice the ginger into small cubes. Set aside. In a bowl, place the softened butter, and with a mixer, fold in the eggs, one by one, add the flour, orange zest and ginger. Pour the mixture in the cake tin and bake for 25 minutes. Then turn out. This cake can be prepared the day before.

Prepare orange marmalade: scald the oranges whole. Cut four into small cubes. Heat the sugar in a saucepan until you obtain a dry caramel. Add the butter and oranges. Cook for 5 minutes, boil and add the water and lemon juice. Simmer until you obtain a marmalade.

Prepare the strussel: preheat the oven to 300 °F (150 °C, gas mark 4). In a bowl, mix all the ingredients until you obtain a stiff dough. Shape into small balls of the same size. Arrange on the baking sheet and bake for 10 minutes, until the outside is crispy and the inside soft.

Decorate the cake: slice the cake horizontally into 3 disks. In a dish, place the first disk, cover with orange marmalade and do the same with the other slices. Finish off with a layer of marmalade and decorate with the slices of cristallized orange. Sprinkle over the strussel.

Wine advice: choose a uncommon wine, a Lillet white wine, which has a flavor of candied fruits and grapefruit.

Valentine's day chocolate cake with pink pralines

RECIPE PAGE 136

This heart-shaped cake has to be prepared with a great deal of love, both for the lightness of the cake and the happiness of the coming year.

Valentine's day chocolate cake with pink pralines

Difficulty : ♜♜♜

Preparation : 30 mn

Cooking time : 30 mn

Standing time : 2 h

Ingredients for two people

100 g shortbread pastry *
50 g dry nougatine *
10 pink pralines
500 g ganache cream*

Sponge cake with almonds and hazelnuts
3 large egg whites
160 g caster sugar
92 g flour
32 g ground almonds
20 g ground hazelnuts
165 nut-brown butter

Pink praline custard
75 g pink pralines
125 g milk
4 egg yolks
1 teaspoon kirsch
4 sheets of gelatine

Heart-shaped cake ring
Greaseproof paper

Prepare sponge cake : beat the egg whites with sugar. Add the flour, almonds, hazelnuts and nut-brown butter. Mix well. Butter the cake ring and place on a baking tray. Pour in the mixture and cover with the greaseproof paper. Preheat the oven to 480 °F (250 °C, gas mark 8). Bake for 12 minutes.

Roll out shortbread pastry* : roll out the shortbread pastry* : cut the dough around the heart-shaped ring. Cut a small heart in the center. Line the baking tray with the greaseproof paper and lay in the dough. Sprinkle the dry nougatine* and crushed pralines over the top. Heat the oven to 310 °F (160 °c, gas mark 4) and bake for 10 minutes.

Prepare pink praline custard : finely crush the pralines. Boil the milk in a pan. Mix the pralines and the egg yolks in a bowl. Pour in the milk. Heat gently, stirring continually. The custard will be ready when the liquid starts thickening, but it must not boil. Remove from the heat and add the kirsh. Soften the gelatine in cold water fold in the mixture. Allow to cool.

Before serving : place the ring on a serving dish, put in the sponge cake, half of the ganache cream* and set aside in the refrigerator for 30 minutes. Add the pink praline custard and top with the remaining ganache cream*. Set aside in the refrigerator for 1 hour and half.

When serving : unmold with great care and top with the shortbread pastry heart.

Wine advice : choose an unusual wine from the Eastern Pyrenees made from the red grenache grape : the Maury.

Mango and pineapple chutney with lychee sorbet

Ingredients for four people

Difficulty: 2/2

100 g shortbread pastry*
50 g dry nougatine*
100 g chocolate shavings
1 teaspoon icing sugar

Lychee sorbet
500 g fresh lychees
125 g caster sugar
85 g water
1/2 lemon juice

Greaseproof paper
Ice-maker

Mango and pineapple chutney
300 g pineapple
300 g mango
35 g dried pears
35 g dried apples
80 g orange juice
60 g lemon juice
1 pinch powdered cinnamon
1 pinch powdered ginger
20 g sherry vinegar
35 g pale raisins
35 g dried currants
35 g dried apricots
Zest of 1 orange
Zest of 1 lime

Preparation: 20 mn

Cooking time: 35 mn

Ice-maker: 30 mn

Prepare the chutney: remove the rind from the pineapple and peel the mango. Dice them into small cubes and do the same with the dried pears and apples. Cook all the ingredients gently in a pan for 20 minutes, until they turn into compote. Set aside in the refrigerator.

Prepare lychee sorbet: wash the fruit and blend. In a saucepan, prepare a syrup with water and sugar, on a medium heat. In a bowl, mix the lychee purée, syrup and lemon juice. Pour into the ice-maker. Set aside in the freezer.

Prepare shortbread pastry rings: roll out the shortbread pastry and cut it into 4 rounds (8 cm in diameter). Cut a 6 cm diameter circle in the center of each to get 4 rings. Line a baking tray with greaseproof paper and place the 4 rings on it. Sprinkle with dry nougatine*. Preheat the oven to 310 °F (160 °C, gas mark 4) and bake for 5 minutes.

When serving: pour a large tablespoon of chutney in the center of each plate. Place a scoop of sorbet on top and then a sweet shortcrust pastry ring. Dust with icing sugar and sprinkle on the chocolate shavings.

Wine advice: choose a Gewurtztraminer, which has flowery and lychee flavours.

Earl Grey Blue Flower ice and sweet pancake

RECIPE PAGE 140

Scented teas come mainly from the traditions of the Orient but bergamot tea was supposedly invented by Earl Grey, a British politician.

Earl Grey Blue Flower ice and sweet pancake

Difficulty: AA

Preparation: 20 mn

Cooking time: 15 mn

Standing time: 1 h

Ice-maker: 30 mn

Ingredients for four people

Pancake batter

220 g flour
1 teaspoon salt
50 g sugar
5 eggs
100 g butter
40 g oil
80 g Grand Marnier
Zest of 1 orange
400 g milk
250 g oil for deep frying
1 teaspoon icing sugar

Tea ice

300 g milk
93 g caster sugar
125 g fresh cream
12,5 g Earl Grey Blue Flower tea
7 egg yolks

Tea flavoured caramel

15 g Earl Grey Blue Flower tea
50 g water
100 g caster sugar

Pastry cutters
Ice-maker

Prepare the pancakes: mix the flour, salt, sugar and eggs in a bowl. In another bowl, blend the melted butter, oil and Grand Marnier. Fold in the first mixture, add the orange zest and milk. Allow to stand for 1 hour. Cook thin pancakes in a 18-20 cm diameter skillet. Allow to cool. With several pastry cutters (of various sizes), cut 6 or 7 cut-outs in each pancake. Deep-fry the pancakes in hot oil. Allow to cool on a paper towel. Sprinkle on caster sugar.

Prepare tea flavoured ice: boil the milk and 50 g sugar in a saucepan. Let the tea infuse for 2.5 minutes in the milk. Mix 43 g caster sugar with the egg yolks in a bowl, beating until the mixture turns frothy. Away from heat, fold the eggs into the milk. Strain. Cook gently, stirring until the mixture coats the back of a spatula. Pour it into the ice-maker. Then set aside in the freezer.

Prepare caramel: let the tea infuse in boiling water for 2.5 minutes. Cook the sugar to obtain a dry caramel. Add the tea and boil until you obtain a thick syrup.

When serving: chill 4 plates in the refrigerator. Place 3 scoops of ice on each plate. Pour some caramel around it. Top with a sweet fried pancake. Dust with icing sugar.

Wine advice: choose a Muscatel from Mireval, in the Montpellier region, which has apricot, peach and honey flavors.

Mendiant, Manjari chocolate and roast bananas

Ingredients for four people

Difficulty: ♜♜

Preparation: 15 mn

Cooking time: 25 mn

200 g sweet shortcrust pastry*
400 g ganache cream*
80 g vanilla juice*
1 lime

Roast bananas
4 bananas
50 g butter
1 teaspoon caster sugar
1 teaspoon rum

Mendiant
100 g caster sugar
100 g double cream
50 g hazelnut
50 g almond
25 g pistachio
30 g orange rind

Cake tin (20 cm in diameter)

Roll out the sweet shortcrust pastry* and line the cake tin. Preheat the oven to 310 °F (160 °C, gas mark 4). Bake for 15 minutes. Remove and set aside on the serving dish.

Prepare roast bananas: fry the sliced bananas with the butter and sugar in a skillet. Deglaze with rum. Leave to cool. Place the fruit in the tart. Warm the ganache cream* and pour into the tart. Set aside in a cool place but not in the refrigerator.

Prepare the mendiant: put the sugar in a pan and cook on a high heat. Add the double cream. You obtain a caramel. Crush the fruit roughly and dice the orange rind. Pour in the caramel and mix well. Make sure the fruit is well-coated. Grease the same cake tin. Pour in the mendiant and allow it to cool. The mendiant will take the shape of the mould.

When serving: top the banana tart with the mendiant. Decorate with thin strips of lime zest and serve with vanilla juice*.

Wine advice: choose a golden sweet wine from the Jura which harmonises with this dessert.

Christmas pear log, cinnamon with wine

Difficulty : ▲▲▲ — INGREDIENTS FOR FOUR PEOPLE

Preparation : 20 mn

Cooking time : 35 mn

PEARS IN SYRUP
6 Williams pears
1/2 l water
250 g sugar

CINNAMON WINE PEARS
6 Williams pears
1 dl blackcurrant liqueur
2 oranges
1 l Brouilly wine
185 g puréed blackcurrant
Juice of 1 lemon
1 clove
80 g caster sugar
1 pinch of powdered cinnamon
1 pinch ginger spice

SPICED SPONGE CAKE
8 egg whites
215 g caster sugar
7 egg yolks
65 g flour
2 teaspoons ginger spice
50 g grounded almond
1 tablespoon icing sugar
Cinnamon sticks
Dried oranges

PEAR CUSTARD
250 g confectioner's custard*
125 g butter
25 g pear *eau-de-vie*

Greaseproof paper

Prepare pears in syrup : peel the fruit, cut them in half and core. Pour the water and sugar into a large pan and add the fruit. Cook until soft (test with a knife blade). Strain. Dice and set aside.

Prepare cinnamon wine pears : peel the fruit and set aside. Cook all the ingrédients in a large saucepan : the blackcurrant liqueur, one orange sliced with its rind, one orange sliced without, the wine, puréed blackcurrants, lemon juice, sugar and spices. Boil and reduce by half on medium heat. Add the whole pears. Once they are cooked, strain, but keep the juice.

Prepare pear custard : mix the confectioner's custard* with the melted butter. Emulsify. Add the pear *eau-de-vie*.

Prepare the sponge cake : beat the egg whites with 100 g caster sugar until stiff. In another bowl, mix the egg yolks and 115 g sugar, beating until the mixture turns white. Fold in the whites gently and add the flour, spices and ground almonds. Mix well. Preheat the oven to 480 °F (250 °C, gas mark 8). Line a baking tray with greaseproof paper and pour in the mixture. Bake for 4 to 5 minutes, until golden. Remove the paper, dust with icing sugar and cover with muslin to keep it soft and damp. Brush the sponge cake with half of the cinnamon wine. Cover with 2/3 of the pear custard and roll tightly. Top the log with the remaining cream and score it with a fork, not forgetting to make a knot or two. Decorate with cinnamon sticks and dried oranges. Set aside in the refrigerator.

When serving: put one sliced pear on each plate and one slice of Christmas log cake. Pour a tablespoon of cinnamon wine around.

Wine advice: a Vouvray, a sweet white Loire wine, vintage 89 or 86.

Appendixes

basic savoury recipes

Appétits

1/2 bunch of chives
Fleur de sel (pure sea salt)
Coarse ground pepper

Chop up the chives. Mix them with the salt and pepper. Set aside.

Beef consommé

For 1 l beef consommé
1 leek
1 carrot
1 tomato
1 stalk of celery
6 eggs
200 g ground beef
2 l beef stock
Salt
Freshly-ground pepper

Wash and finely slice the vegetables. Whisk the egg whites briefly and fold in the meat and vegetables. Add about ten ice cubes. Season. Boil the beef stock. Pour gradually over the mixture and mix well. Boil. When the egg whites coagulate, they form a thick layer on the surface. Make a hole in it when boiling begins. Allow to simmer for 20 minutes. Remove from heat and let it stand for 15 minutes. Line a strainer with a cloth and strain the stock. Wring the cloth. Set aside.

Bouquet garni

1 green part of leek
1 sprig of thyme
1 bay leaf
1 sprig of parsley
1 sprig of celery

Wash all the ingredients, then tie them with cooking string into a bouquet.

Candied tomatoes

For 6 tomatoes
6 large tomatoes
1 clove of garlic
4 tablespoons olive oil
Salt
Freshly-ground pepper

Scald the tomatoes for a few seconds, then dip them in cold water and peel them. Remove the seeds. Put them in an ovenproof dish. Cover about three quarters with olive oil. Season and sprinkle on the chopped garlic. Preheat the oven to 160 °F (70 °C, gas mark 2) and bake for 1 hour and a half.

Chicken stock

For 1 l chicken stock
2 kg chicken carcass
600 g carrots
450 g onions
1 stalk of celery
1 calf's foot
1 sprig of thyme
1 bay leaf
3 l water
Salt
Freshly-ground pepper

Peel the vegetables and cut them into large pieces. Put all the ingredients into a large pan. Reduce by half, on a low heat. Skim off the fat and strain. Set aside in the refrigerator.

Chicken gravy

For 1/2 l chicken gravy
6 shallots
1 onion
1 kg chicken carcass
10 cl olive oil
3 sprigs of thyme
1 bay leaf
1 sprig of parsley
1 l chicken stock*
10 cl dry white wine
Salt
Freshly-ground pepper
Ground pepper

Peel the shallots and onion and cut them into a *mirepoix*. Crush the carcass and brown it with olive oil in a large pan. Add the *mirepoix*, herbs and ground pepper. Deglaze with the white wine. Add the stock and cook for 25 minutes. Strain and reduce until you obtain 1/2 l gravy. Season.

Crushed tomatoes

For 600 g crushed tomatoes

Scald the tomatoes for few seconds, then dip them in cold water and peel them. Halve them and press to remove seeds and water. Cut the pulp in a *mirepoix* and drain for 1 hour. Set aside.

Lamb gravy

For 1 l lamb gravy
3.5 kg lamb bones
1.2 kg carrots
600 g onions
1 head of garlic/1 calf's foot
1 sprig of thyme/1 bay leaf
2 tablespoons tomato concentrate
4 tablespoons olive oil
3 l water
Salt
Freshly-ground pepper

Brown the bones in a large pan. Peel and coarsely dice them. Add all the ingredients to the pan. Cook gently for 3 hours. Skim off the fat and strain. Set aside in the refrigerator.

Langoustine stock

For 250 g langoustine stock
8 large *langoustines*
1 carrot
1 leek
1 onion
90 g butter

Shell the *langoustines* and set aside the tails. Peel the vegetables and cut them into large pieces. Put the crushed *langoustine* heads, water and vegetables into a pan and boil. Reduce by three quarters. Strain. Add the butter and heat again. Reduce by half. Keep warm.

Meat glaze

For 1/4 l meat glaze
3 shallots
1 tablespoon butter
100 g ox cheek
1 bouquet garni*
1 l veal stock*

Heat the chopped shallots with the butter. Add the ox cheek and brown well. Add the *bouquet garni** and the stock. Reduce by three quarters on a low heat. Strain. Set aside.

Mussel gravy

For 1/2 l mussel gravy
1/2 l dry white wine
1 head of garlic
1 sprig of thyme
1 bay leaf
1 kg mussels
8 tablespoons cream
80 g butter

Pour the wine into a large pan. Add the crushed garlic, bay leaf and the chopped onion. Reduce by half on a high heat. Add the mussels and cook for 1 minute. Drain the mussels and strain the stock. Pour the stock into a pan and add the cream and the butter. Reduce by half. Set aside. Shell the mussels and set aside.

Olive Oil *Béarnaise*

For 300 g *béarnaise*
250 g olive oil
2 shallots/20 g tarragon
2 dl dry white wine
5 g ground pepper
2 dl vinegar/6 eggs
10 g chervil
3 tablespoons of parsley
Salt
Freshly-ground pepper

Heat the olive oil. Gently heat the chopped shallots, tarragon, white wine, pepper and vinegar. Reduce. Pour it into a *bain-marie*, and add the egg yolks and half a glass of water, beat with a whisk until you obtain a thick cream. Add the warm olive oil and strain. Season. Add chopped chervil and parsley. Keep warm in the double boiler.

Parmesan Crisp

For 4 parmesan crisps
150 g parmesan
Greaseproof paper
1 tablespoon olive oil
Freshly-ground pepper

Grate the parmesan. Brush the paper with the olive oil and line the baking tray. Preheat the oven to 60 °F (240 °C, gas mark 8). Bake for a few moments. Remove the paper with great care. Leave to cool.

Red wine sauce with shallots

For 1 l red wine sauce
1,3 kg ox cheek/1,5 l red wine
100 g onions/50 g carrots
1/2 stick of celery
1 *bouquet garni**
2 tomatoes
1/2 l veal stock*
3 tablespoons olive oil

Brown the ox cheek with olive oil in a large pot. Peel and coarsely dice all the vegetables. Add all ingredients to the pot and reduce by half, for 1 hour on a low heat. Strain. Set aside in the refrigerator.

Veal gravy

For 1 l veal gravy
600 g shoulder of lamb
1 leek/1 carrot
1 fennel bulb
1/4 head of celeriac
1/2 calf's foot
1 bouquet garni*
3 tablespoons olive oil
1 l veal stock*
Peppercorns

Peel the leek, carrot, fennel and celeriac; and cut them into a *mirepoix*. Brown the diced meat with olive oil. Add the vegetables, calf's foot, the *bouquet garni** and the stock. Reduce by half on a low heat. Strain. Set aside.

Veal stock

For 1/2 l veal stock
1.6 kg veal bones
400 g carrots/200 g onions
1 stalk of celery/1 calf's foot
1 sprig of thyme/1 bay leaf
2 tablespoons tomato concentrate
4 tablespoons olive oil/2 l water
Salt
Freshly-ground pepper

Brown the bones in oil in a large saucepan. Peel and dice the vegetables. Add all the ingrédients to the pan and cook gently for 3 hours. Skim off the fat and strain. Set aside in the refrigerator.

basic sweet recipes

Basic ganache cream

FOR 1.1 KG GANACHE CREAM
420 g chocolate
500 g single cream
175 g butter

Crush the chocolate in a bowl. Boil the cream and pour it on the chocolate. Stir until you obtain a smooth cream. Fold in the butter. Mix well.

Brioche pastry dough

FOR 125 G BRIOCHE PASTRY DOUGH
125 g flour
2 g baker's yeast
1 egg
20 g caster sugar
3 g salt
65 g butter

Make a well in the flour and mix in the yeast. Add the egg, sugar and salt. Knead until you obtain an « elastic » dough. Fold in the butter. Put the dough in a bowl and cover with a cloth. Leave to stand at room temperature for 1 hour. Knead again and set aside in the refrigerator the night before it is used.

Confectioner's Custard

FOR 800 G CUSTARD
2 eggs
4 egg yolks
125 g caster sugar
50 g flour
10 g cornstarch
1/2 l full fat milk
1 vanilla pod

Mix the eggs, the egg yolks and the sugar in a bowl. Add the flour and the cornstarch. Stir until you obtain a creamy mixture. Boil the milk with the vanilla pod. Mix it with the egg mixture. Cook over a low heat, stirring until it boils, to obtain a thick, smooth cream. Pour into a bowl and leave to cool. Set aside in the refrigerator.

Dry nougatine

FOR 500 G DRY NOUGATINE
165 g glucose
250 g ready-made white icing (*fondant*)
20 g butter
13 g powdered almonds
Zest of 1 orange
Zest of 1 lemon
Greaseproof paper

Put the glucose and icing into a pan and cook until it turns golden. Add all the ingredients. Stir. Pour the mixture on to the paper and allow to cool. Finely crush and store in an airtight tin.

Lime julienne

5 limes
250 g caster sugar
250 g water

With a potato peeler, peel the limes. Cut them into very thin strips. Make a syrup with water and sugar. Add the lime peel. Cook for 15 minutes on a low heat.

Shortbread pastry

For 400 g dough
10 g flour
40 g ground almonds
60 g icing sugar
120 g butter
1 lemon
1 orange
1 egg

Make a well in the flour. Add the ground almonds, the sugar, the butter and the rind from the lemon and orange. Mix and fold in the egg. Knead until you obtain a supple dough. Wrap in cling film and set aside in the refrigerator for a few hours before use.

Sweet shortcrust pastry

For 400 g dough
250 g flour
100 g butter
100 g caster sugar
2 eggs
10 g baking powder
1 teaspoon vanilla extract

Make a well in the flour. Add the softened butter and the sugar. Add the eggs, baking powder and vanilla. Knead the dough with the palm of your hand until you obtain an even dough. Wrap in the cling film and set aside in the refrigerator for 3 to 4 hours before use.

Vanilla juice

For 800 g vanilla juice
8 vanilla pods
1/2 l water
250 g caster sugar
Juice of 3 lemons

Split the vanilla pods and scrape out the seeds. Boil the water and add the sugar, the pods and seeds. Allow to simmer for 10 minutes. Add the lemon juice. Set aside.

culinary terms

Blanch: dip food in salted and boiling water. The boiling time should not exceed 1 minute and half.

Brunoise: finely diced vegetables (cubes of about 5 mm).

Clarified butter: slowly melt the butter and remove the foam as well as impurities and the whey.

Deglaze: pour water, wine or brandy over meat dripping to obtain a gravy.

Julienne: vegetables which are sliced, then cut into very thin strips.

Mirepoix: vegetables which are diced into cubes of about 1 centimeter.

Nut-brown butter: slowly brown the butter in a skillet until it becomes nut-colored.

Quenelle: to obtain a *quenelle*, use two tablespoons and form it into a *quenelle* shape.

Reduce: reduce the volume of a liquid or a sauce by boiling.

Scald: dip in boiling water for a few seconds.

Shred: cut in narrow strips, then dice into very small pieces.

table of recipes

starters

fish

meat

desserts

acknowledgements

We would like to thank the "Société Nouvelle d'exploitation de la Tour Eiffel" and the Elior Group for permitting us to publish this book.

We would also like to thank the S.N.T.E. for putting its archives at our disposal and allowing us to use the photographs from its private collection, on pages 14, 15, 16, and 19. Special thanks to GMB.

Alain Reix would like to thank his entire team in the kitchens of Jules Verne and particularly:
Fabrice Seigner, his assistant;
Philippe Rollando, his pastry chef.
And for their collaboration in making this book:
Amar Chebrek, chef-sommelier;
Arnaud Tachi and the the dining-room staff.
Edouard Sicot was assisted by Massimo Pessina for the photography.

Printed in France by Pollina - n° 81824A
N° édition : 080311-01 — Dépôt légal : novembre 2000